The Walter Lynwood Fleming Lectures in Southern History

LOUISIANA STATE UNIVERSITY

Lincoln, the South, and Slavery

HON. ABRAM LINCOLN, OF ILLINOIS, REPUBLICAN CANDIDATE FOR PRESIDENT.

[PHOTOGRAPHED BY BRADY.]

LINCOLN,
the South, and Slavery

The Political Dimension

Robert W. Johannsen

LOUISIANA STATE UNIVERSITY PRESS
Baton Rouge

Designer: Patricia Douglas Crowder
Typeface: Linotron 202 Janson
Typesetter: Graphic Composition, Inc.

LIBRARY OF CONGRESS CATALOGING-IN-PUBLICATION DATA

Johannsen, Robert Walter, 1925–
   Lincoln, the South, and slavery : the political dimension / Robert
W. Johannsen.
      p.   cm. — (Walter Lynwood Fleming lectures in southern
history)
   Includes index.
   ISBN 0-8071-1637-8 (cloth).   ISBN 0-8071-1887-7 (paper).
   1. United States—Politics and government—1849–1861.   2. Lincoln,
Abraham, 1809–1865—Political career before 1861.   3. Slavery—
United States—Anti-slavery movements.   I. Title.   II. Series.
E415.7.J685   1991
973.7'092—dc20
                                                                90-48474
                                                                CIP

Chapter 4 was delivered in 1989 as the Twelfth R. Gerald McMurtry Lecture, sponsored by the Louis A. Warren Lincoln Library and Museum, Fort Wayne, Indiana,
and subsequently published as a pamphlet by the library.

Frontispiece reproduced from *Harper's Weekly*, May 26, 1860, p. 321.

The paper in this book meets the guidelines for permanence and durability of the
Committee on Production Guidelines for Book Longevity of the Council on Library
Resources.∞

Louisiana Paperback Edition, 1993
02   01   00   5   4   3

for
Andriah, Katherine, Ryan, and Stuart

Contents

Preface

"But for his election in 1860," David Donald has written, "Lincoln's name would appear in our history books as that of a minor Illinois politician who unsuccessfully debated with Stephen A. Douglas."[1] Few would dispute the fact that the figure of the Little Giant was closely linked with Lincoln's brief antislavery career prior to his election as president. After so many years devoted to a study of Stephen A. Douglas, it was inevitable that I should be attracted to Douglas' longtime political adversary, if only to understand the nature of Douglas' opposition and to be able thereby to place Douglas' position in a broader context. The opportunity to examine Lincoln's role in the politics of the slavery question from 1854 to 1860 was offered when I was so graciously invited to deliver the Walter Lynwood Fleming Lectures in Southern History at Louisiana State University. For that invitation, I am deeply indebted to John Loos, whose interest in and support of my work have meant a great deal to me, and to the members of the history department at LSU. The generous and congenial hospitality extended to me during my visit to the Baton Rouge campus exceeded all expectations. The lectures, in a somewhat revised and expanded form, follow as the Introduction and Chapters 1–3.

1. David Donald, "A. Lincoln, Politician," in Donald, *Lincoln Reconsidered: Essays on the Civil War Era* (New York, 1956), 57.

Chapter 4 was initially delivered as the Twelfth R. Gerald Mc-Murtry Lecture, sponsored by the Louis A. Warren Lincoln Library and Museum in Fort Wayne, Indiana. For that invitation, as well as for the warm reception I encountered in Fort Wayne and for the helpful advice and assistance so freely offered on other occasions, I am indebted to Mark E. Neely, Jr., Director of the library and museum and a distinguished Lincoln scholar in his own right. Mark has generously granted permission to reprint the McMurtry Lecture in this volume.

Anyone who embarks on a study of Abraham Lincoln, I have learned, must first come to terms with the Lincoln myth. The effort to penetrate the crust of legend that surrounds Lincoln, to view Lincoln in something other than presentist terms, is both a formidable and intimidating task. Lincoln, it seems, requires special considerations that are denied to other figures of his generation. One need not subscribe to M. E. Bradford's harsh strictures against Lincoln to agree with his observation that Lincoln has been placed "beyond the reach of ordinary historical inquiry and assessment." The rules of historical evidence, one other recent writer has suggested, "have only a limited value in assessing a national hero such as Lincoln." Lincoln is almost literally "beyond history." [2]

Still, I feel more convinced than ever that there is value in trying to see the prepresidential Lincoln in the way his own generation, including Douglas, saw him. The political dimension to Lincoln's antislavery position, as it evolved from the passage of the Kansas-Nebraska Act to his election as president, has not been sufficiently appreciated. Was Lincoln any the less a politician than Douglas? I don't think so. This does not mean that one must question the sincerity of Lincoln's antislavery convictions; rather, what it means is that it is important to examine and emphasize the way in which Lincoln's particular expression of these convictions was shaped and directed by political exigencies and motivations. Lincoln was no crusader (indeed, he rather distrusted those who were, such as the abolitionists); for him, the key matter was always the *politics* of slav-

2. M. E. Bradford, "The Lincoln Legacy: A Long View," in Bradford, *Remembering Who We Are: Observations of a Southern Conservative* (Athens, Ga., 1985), 143; Barbara Burns Petrick, "Lincoln as Myth: Beyond Analysis by Historians," New York *Times*, February 9, 1986, Sec. 11, p. 28.

ery. Given that, in what follows I wish to stress the importance of studying this political dimension of the antislavery convictions Lincoln held from that moment in 1854 when he confessed that slavery was no longer a minor issue with him; clearly, however, the following chapters only scratch the surface of the issue.

For assistance in searching newspaper files, journals and periodicals, and as much of the vast Lincoln literature that time allowed, I am indebted to Brian Kenny, doctoral candidate at the University of Illinois. For their support of this project I am grateful to the members of the Graduate Research Board of the University of Illinois and to the Arnold O. Beckman Research Endowment. For their guidance and helpful suggestions, I am also indebted to Les Phillabaum, Director, and to Margaret Fisher Dalrymple, Editor-in-Chief, of the Louisiana State University Press. Finally, once again, I must acknowledge the continuing encouragement of my wife, Lois.

Lincoln, the South, and Slavery

Introduction

In the spring of 1945, James Garfield Randall delivered the Walter Lynwood Fleming Lectures in Southern History at Louisiana State University, the eighth lecturer in the series. His theme was "Lincoln and the South," his text a statement from Fleming's small book on Reconstruction, *The Sequel of Appomattox*, in which Fleming suggested that Lincoln "appreciated conditions in the South" better than most Union leaders. It was the heyday of the so-called revisionist interpretation of the causes of the Civil War, and Randall was one of its chief exponents. His pioneering textbook, *The Civil War and Reconstruction*, in which he placed a pro-Southern cast on that tragic conflict, was less than a decade old, and his monumental two-volume work on *Lincoln the President* was already at his publishers. It was no surprise that he should use the opportunity offered by the Fleming Lectures to point out that the war came because of misunderstanding, false propaganda, overbearing agitation, and blundering. One reviewer later observed that Randall delivered his lectures before what must have been "highly sympathetic audiences at Louisiana State."[1]

Randall, regarded today as the "greatest Lincoln scholar of all

1. James G. Randall, *Lincoln and the South* (Baton Rouge, 1946), 1–2, 86; John David Smith, "James G. Randall," in *Dictionary of Literary Biography*, ed. Clyde N. Wilson (Detroit, 1983), XVII, 375–76; Arthur Meier Schlesinger, Jr., Review of Randall's *Lincoln and the South*, in *Nation*, June 15, 1946, p. 725.

time," explored those elements in Lincoln's thought that touched the South, both before and during the Civil War, and integrated Lincoln into the revisionist view by arguing that he was much closer to the South than he was to the antislavery radicals in his own party. Lincoln, Randall noted, was bound to the South by ties that were both fundamental and emotional. His birth, his speech, his law partners, and his wife all linked him with the South. His hero was the border South's great statesman, Henry Clay. Randall contended, moreover, that Lincoln's political views were uniquely Southern in character, shaped by a Southern environment, and inspired by Southern leaders. He was "at one with the large and influential brotherhood of Southern Whigs." The key to Randall's approach to Lincoln was in his belief that Lincoln could be understood only in terms of a "courageous and undaunted liberalism," a liberalism, as he asserted in his lectures, that bore Southern characteristics. Lincoln, he maintained, was a Southern liberal in the mold of John Taylor of Caroline, George Mason, and Thomas Jefferson. Focusing on the wartime Lincoln, Randall pointed out that his policies toward the border slave states and his programs for emancipation and reconstruction distinguished him as a man who knew the South, who respected Southern rights, and who was considerate of Southern interests.[2]

Randall was not the first nor would he be the last to view Lincoln as a Southerner in mind and character. Lincoln himself often alluded to a Southern side of his nature, attributing his "finer qualities" to his Southern parentage and upbringing, and pleading his Southern origins as an excuse for an occasional indelicate reference to blacks. His speech was interspersed with Southern idioms and his accent was unmistakably Southern. Lincoln frequently addressed Southerners during his prepresidential career, not because he knew they were listening or were even in a position to hear his words but rather to convey to his Northern audiences the image of one who knew and understood the South. The tactic was not unsuccessful, for many of his followers felt that his Southern credentials gave him advantages

2. Mark E. Neely, Jr., *The Abraham Lincoln Encyclopedia* (New York, 1982), 255; Don E. Fehrenbacher, *The Changing Image of Lincoln in American Historiography* (Oxford, 1968), 17; James G. Randall, *Lincoln the Liberal Statesman* (New York, 1947), ix; Randall, *Lincoln and the South*, 9, 11, 16–17, 25–26, 47–48.

that Northern-born politicians could not match. As a Southern man, it was said, he was that sort of Republican who would not be easily seduced from his convictions. He was better able to recognize the evils of slavery and to measure the sinister designs of the Slave Power. On the other hand, his Southern experience not only made him an unusually effective spokesman for the Republican party, but also, as some suggested, would make him a president who would be acceptable and sympathetic to the South.[3]

Following his death, Lincoln's Southernness became a recurring theme in the literature. Walt Whitman described him as "essentially, in personnel and character, a Southern contribution." Another wrote that there was something "essentially southern" about Lincoln, especially his "warm-heartedness" and "fun-loving rowdiness." Thomas Nelson Page found the key to Lincoln's passion for preserving the Union in the fact of his Southern birth. Then there were those who felt that such a great man could not have been sired by so lowly a person as Thomas Lincoln. There had to be a higher Southern pedigree lurking somewhere in the shadows, perhaps a tidewater planter or the scion of one of the South's ancient families. The list of those who were alleged to have fathered Lincoln grew apace, including Samuel Davis (which would make Lincoln the half brother of Jefferson Davis), Patrick Henry (although Henry died ten years before Lincoln was born), Henry Clay (from whom it was said Lincoln got his height), and John C. Calhoun (Lincoln being the result of a misadventure with a barmaid named Nancy Hanks). If these speculations proved hard to accept, there was the claim of one biographer that Lincoln and Robert E. Lee were cousins.[4]

3. William H. Herndon and Jesse W. Weik, *Herndon's Life of Lincoln*, ed. Paul M. Angle (Cleveland, 1949), 2–3; Randall, *Lincoln and the South*, 2–3; Speech at Belleville, Illinois, October 18, 1856, in *The Collected Works of Abraham Lincoln*, ed. Roy P. Basler et al. (9 vols.; New Brunswick, N.J., 1954), II, 379–80; New York *Tribune*, June 26, 1858; Baltimore *Patriot*, quoted in Springfield *Illinois State Journal*, September 26, 1860.

4. Walt Whitman, "Death of Abraham Lincoln, April 14, 1879," in *The Complete Writings of Walt Whitman*, ed. Oscar Lovell Triggs (10 vols.; New York, 1902), II, 240; The Southerner, "Lincoln and Lee," *South Atlantic Quarterly*, XXVI (January, 1927), 9–10; Thomas Nelson Page, "On Lincoln" (Address delivered February 12, 1909, in Washington, D.C.), presented in Frederic Haines Curtiss, "A Southerner's View of Abraham Lincoln," *Proceedings of the Massachusetts Historical Society*, LXIX (October, 1947–May, 1950), 314; J. G. de Roulhac Hamilton, "The Many-Sired Lincoln,"

Equally eccentric was the portrayal of Lincoln by Thomas Dixon, the North Carolina novelist whose book *The Clansman* furnished D. W. Griffith with inspiration for his movie *The Birth of a Nation.* In 1913, Dixon published *The Southerner: A Romance of the Real Lincoln*, a tedious work with an improbable story line, in which Lincoln was described as the quintessential Southerner, a man who "never breathed anything but Southern air and ideals." "It's in his blood," wrote Dixon. The proof was in Lincoln's belief in the inequality of the black and white races and in his conviction that peace and harmony could never be achieved until all blacks should be separated from white society. Lincoln's "prophetic soul," Dixon claimed, "had pierced the future."[5]

It is not my intention to become involved in the question of whether or not Lincoln was a genuine Southerner. Few if any historians today, I suspect, would accept Randall's premise. Lincoln's most recent biographer, for example, has conceded Lincoln's exposure to Southern ideas and influences, but he rejects the notion that it directed his thought as an antislavery leader and as a wartime president. Richard N. Current, in putting to rest what he calls the "Lincoln-the-Southerner myth," has insisted that Lincoln's ideas and ideals were antithetical to the "traditionalism" that characterized the South, and that Lincoln himself knew it.[6]

Although he continued to feel that he understood the South and Southern thinking, Lincoln must have been aware that he had lost his Southern credentials well before he ran for the presidency. The 1860 election merely clinched it. During the campaign, he responded to an invitation to visit his native Kentucky with the questions: "But would it be safe? Would not the people Lynch me?" When the press chided him for being afraid to express his opinions

---

American Mercury, V (June, 1925), 129–35; William E. Barton, "Abraham Lincoln Was a Lee," *Good Housekeeping*, LXXXVIII (January, 1929), 199.

5. Thomas Dixon, *The Southerner: A Romance of the Real Lincoln* (New York, 1913), 266, 543. Dixon later incorporated the same point of view in his play *A Man of the People: A Drama of Abraham Lincoln* (New York, 1920).

6. Stephen B. Oates, "'My Dissatisfied Fellow Countrymen': Abraham Lincoln and the Slaveholding South," in *Essays on Southern History Written in Honor of Barnes F. Lathrop*, ed. Gary W. Gallagher (Austin, 1980), 97–116; Richard Nelson Current, "Lincoln the Southerner," in Current, *Speaking of Abraham Lincoln: The Man and His Meaning for Our Times* (Urbana, 1983), 146–71.

in a slave state, he pleaded that he meant his response to be taken "playfully." It must have been clear to him, however, that a widening gulf had opened between him and the South. Following Lincoln's election as president, one Southerner declared Lincoln was nothing more than a "Southern renegade—spewed out of Kentucky into Illinois" and a traitor to the section of his birth.[7]

Lincoln should have been exceptionally well-informed about Southern attitudes, concerns, and convictions. A voracious reader of newspapers, to such an extent that his wife became annoyed with him, he regularly received a number of papers from the slave states; two of those papers, the Charleston *Mercury* and the Richmond *Enquirer*, he believed to be the South's "greatest leading presses." Furthermore, Lincoln was a careful reader of the *Southern Literary Messenger*, to which his wife subscribed, an important medium of Southern cultural expression.[8] The fact is, however, he was not as well-informed as one might have expected. As his political career flourished, he became increasingly indifferent toward Southern sentiments, and during the 1860 election campaign seemed not to have comprehended the seriousness of Southern fears and threats. Lincoln did not seem to appreciate the nature or depth of the South's commitment to slavery (except perhaps at the very beginning of his antislavery career in 1854); he appeared to be unaware of the extent to which the institution was woven through the fabric of Southern civilization; and he paid little attention to a Southern concept of republicanism that would offer protection against a hostile majority outside the South. Where the South was concerned, Lincoln's vision was myopic.

Lincoln was a man of his times, and the times did not always induce clear, careful, and profound observation. Stephen A. Douglas aptly observed of Lincoln, "[He] is eminently a man of the atmosphere which surrounds him." America's midcentury years were years of contradiction and paradox, and it is no denigration of Lin-

7. Lincoln to Samuel Haycraft, June 4, 1860, Lincoln to George C. Fogg, August 16, 1860, in *Collected Works*, IV, 69–70, 96–97; New York *Herald*, August 13, 14, 1860; Charleston *Courier*, November 21, 1860.

8. Herndon and Weik, *Herndon's Life of Lincoln*, 93, 293; Lincoln to John E. Rosette, February 20, 1857, in *Collected Works*, II, 390; Springfield *Illinois Daily Journal*, November 7, 1854; Herbert J. Edwards and John E. Hankins, *Lincoln the Writer: The Development of His Literary Style* (Orono, Maine, 1962), 54–55.

coln to suggest that these same qualities were reflected in his think-ing. He ought not be faulted for not knowing what we today know only through hindsight. Yet Lincoln's complexity was often puzzling to his contemporaries. He was given, for example, to what has been termed "enigmatic silences." To his law partner, who knew him bet-ter than most, Lincoln was the "most secretive—reticent—shut-mouthed man that ever existed." To know his thoughts was not easy then, and it is even more difficult now. "You had to *guess* at the man after years of acquaintance," observed William H. Herndon, "and then you must look long and keenly before you *guessed* or you would make an ass of yourself." His silences were deliberate, for Lincoln himself took pride in the fact that he was a man who could hold his tongue. To try to follow the thread of his arguments through the tangled skein of sectional politics in the 1850s can be an exasperating and frustrating experience, for just when you think you have him pinned down to a line of argument, he shifts his ground and slips out of your grasp.[9]

The task is not made easier by Lincoln's avowedly political na-ture. His ambition for political office was intense, a "little engine that knew no rest." That he was a master politician at a time when politics had become a tumultuous and often violent spectator-sport has long been recognized by those who have studied his career. Herndon observed that those who think Lincoln "calmly sat down and gathered his robes about him, waiting for the people to call him," are grossly mistaken. On the contrary, he "was always calcu-lating, and always planning ahead." A devout and dedicated party man, he was thoroughly attuned to the single-minded partisanship of the Jackson era.[10]

Lincoln had a natural feel for politics that demonstrated itself in virtually everything he touched, but it was in his response to the

9. Stephen A. Douglas, quoted in Robert W. Johannsen, *Stephen A. Douglas* (New York, 1973), 845; Richard N. Current, *The Lincoln Nobody Knows* (New York, 1958), 12; William H. Herndon to J. E. Remsberg, September, 1887, quoted in Herndon and Weik, *Herndon's Life of Lincoln*, xxxix; Remarks at the Monongahela House, Pitts-burgh, Pennsylvania, February 14, 1861, in *Collected Works*, IV, 209.

10. Herndon and Weik, *Herndon's Life of Lincoln*, 304. For Lincoln as a politician, see also Current, *The Lincoln Nobody Knows*, 187–213; and Richard Hofstadter, *The American Political Tradition and the Men Who Made It* (New York, 1948), 92–134.

issue of slavery from 1854 to 1860 that his political nature became most manifest. Nearly all of his public statements on the slavery question prior to his election as president were delivered with political intent and for political effect. As the sectional crisis deepened and his political career brightened, he brought into play all the strategies that seemed to be required at any given moment—noncommittalism, evasion, ambiguity, silence—and achieved a success that surprised even himself.

This is not to suggest that Lincoln's response lacked principle. It obviously did not. While ambition drove Lincoln hard, Don Fehrenbacher has pointed out, it was an ambition "leavened by moral conviction." The combination of morality and expediency, ever present in Lincoln, simply adds to the complexity of the man. Lincoln was apparently aware that some might misconstrue his motives, for he repeatedly (and not always convincingly) disavowed his personal ambition. He was, he said, moved by "something higher than an anxiety for office." There is no reason to doubt his sincerity. At the same time, however, he admitted that he was as "selfish" as the "average of men." While he would insist that the dispute over slavery was more than an "agitation of office seekers and ambitious Northern politicians," his own "anxiety for office" was seldom far from his thoughts.[11] The precise contours of his arguments at any one time or place were influenced as much by his reading of the political exigencies and by his concern for his own and his party's interests, as they were by his moral convictions. Indeed, the two forces—morality and politics—merged, for Lincoln ultimately argued that the moral character of the republic depended upon the political success of the Republican party and specifically upon his own election to office. For that reason, party loyalty and regularity were for him always moral obligations. There is no doubt that Lincoln's principle served him well politically, that in his hands the moral imperative generated by the slavery issue became a powerful political weapon.

My purpose in the following chapters is to explore, in what can

11. Don E. Fehrenbacher, *Prelude to Greatness: Lincoln in the 1850's* (Stanford, 1962), 161; Speech at Lewistown, Illinois, August 17, 1858, Seventh and Last Debate with Stephen A. Douglas at Alton, Illinois, October 15, 1858, in *Collected Works*, II, 547, III, 310.

only be a very preliminary fashion, the political dimension to Lincoln's evolving antislavery position during his prepresidential years, or what may be called his "second political career," from his dramatic resumption of an active political life in 1854 to his election as president in 1860. Although he insisted in 1860 that his position had not changed since its first expression six years before, the fact is that it had. Taking into account the backing and filling that is common to all political discourse, it seems clear that Lincoln's argument against slavery and his prescription for dealing with it moved from what he initially labeled a middle-ground stand to a more radical position, and that this movement was directly influenced by the exigencies of a fluid and often confused and uncertain political situation. It was not an easy time for a politically ambitious individual, but Lincoln was more fortunate than many others. His skills carried him through to a success he had hardly dreamed of at the beginning, but while he achieved the advancement he sought in the North, he aroused a spirit of alienation in the South that augured ill for the future of the Union.

If the name of Lincoln's principal longtime adversary and political opponent, Stephen A. Douglas, should at times share my attention, it is because I strongly believe that no other individual (not even Henry Clay) exerted so extraordinarily important an influence on the shaping of Lincoln's attitudes toward slavery and the South. Virtually every major public statement Lincoln made between 1854 and 1860 was inspired by a previous statement or action by Douglas, a fact Lincoln readily admitted. It was impossible, he said in 1859, for him to speak of politics "without associating Judge Douglas with it." It was Douglas who set Lincoln's agenda, and it was Douglas who defined the issues, making it possible for Lincoln to acquire a reputation outside his home state. It was, in other words, Douglas who "put Lincoln in a posture to gain national notice." A friendly editor, in the midst of the 1858 senatorial campaign in Illinois, likened Lincoln to Byron, "who woke up one morning to find himself famous." That fame, he told Lincoln, was acquired "by entering the lists against a 'Giant.'" Although Douglas was only a Little Giant, standing five feet four inches tall, or a full twelve inches shorter than Lincoln, his coattails were long enough to carry Lincoln into the front rank of American politicians. A Cincinnati newspaper put it more bluntly: Lincoln "is a symbol of private and party enmity to the Senator of Illinois" and owes "his entire significance to that antagonism. Without Douglas, Lincoln would be nothing."[12]

The two men reflected divergent points of view in the political culture of nineteenth-century America—Lincoln the latitudinarian concepts of national centralization and authority, Douglas the strict constructionist emphasis on local self-government and states' rights; Lincoln the Whig suspicious of human nature and distrustful of mass democracy, Douglas the Jacksonian with an almost transcendental faith in the popular will. They had been sparring against one another in local political contests since the 1830s. While Douglas experienced a meteoric rise to a position of national leadership in the Democratic party, Lincoln's career fell short of expectations. He bemoaned the fact that with him, "the race of ambition [had] been a failure—a flat failure," while the career of Douglas was "one of splendid success." Although Lincoln was more pessimistic in assessing his career than he needed to be, the contrast between himself and Douglas, so often drawn, bothered him. It was Douglas' "continual assumption of superiority on account of his elevated position," he told a friend, that was especially vexing.

As their rivalry grew more intense in the last years of the 1850s, their relationship became strained. Their differences were sharply defined, for they stood in strong disagreement on the nature of the sectional crisis, its urgency, and the danger it presented to the unity of the nation. Each professed respect for the other, but their tributes were barbed. "Mr. Lincoln," remarked Douglas during the Illinois debates, "is a kind-hearted, amiable, good-natured gentleman, . . . a fine lawyer, possesses high ability, and there is no objection to him, except the monstrous revolutionary doctrines . . . which he conscientiously entertains." Two years later, Lincoln spoke of Douglas' "great hardihood, pertinacity and magnetic power," but added that

12. Speech at Indianapolis, Indiana, September 19, 1859, in *Collected Works*, III, 463; Waldo W. Braden, *Abraham Lincoln, Public Speaker* (Baton Rouge, 1988), 35; Charles H. Ray to Lincoln, July 27, 1858, in Abraham Lincoln Papers, Library of Congress (microfilm); Cincinnati *Enquirer*, September, 1859, in Herbert Mitgang, ed., *Lincoln as They Saw Him* (New York, 1956), 141–42.

of all men he had ever known, Douglas had the "most audacity in maintaining an untenable position."[13]

Douglas, the spokesman of the Northern Democracy, born in Vermont and educated in the "burned-over district" of upstate New York, became the foil for Lincoln's arguments against slavery. For Lincoln, he was the personification of the slaveholding South, the very essence of the proslavery position, a leader in promoting the sinister designs of the Slave Power, and a conspirator not only against the founding ideals of the republic but against God's divine law as well. Douglas represented all that was reprehensible about the South. Indeed, Lincoln insisted that Douglas was a better friend to the slaveholding interest than were the Southerners themselves, and at one point he urged the South to support him for the presidency in 1860. According to Lincoln, the South could find no better candidate. Lincoln brushed aside the quarrel between Douglas and the South that resulted in the complete rejection of the Illinois senator as a reliable defender of Southern interests. It was, he said, a mere quibble, of no consequence to the course of political events.

On one of the rare occasions when Lincoln addressed the South directly (in this instance, Kentucky, although he hoped his words would have a wider impact), he stressed the importance of Douglas to the South, at the same time revealing the significance of the Little Giant to his own career. The South's only hope, he explained, lay with Douglas in the North, for it was Douglas who molded Northern public opinion to Southern ends. It was indispensable to the South to "retain support and strength from the Free States," and it was only Douglas who could provide that support and strength. "If you do not get this support and this strength from the Free States," he declared, "you are in the minority, and you are beaten at once."[14]

Beat Douglas, Lincoln told his Northern audiences, and you beat

13. Fragment on Stephen A. Douglas, December 1856?, in *Collected Works*, II, 383; Joseph Gillespie to Herndon, January 31, 1866, in Emanuel Hertz, *The Hidden Lincoln: From the Letters and Papers of William H. Herndon* (New York, 1938), 288; Douglas at Springfield, July 17, 1858, in Paul M. Angle, ed., *Created Equal? The Complete Lincoln-Douglas Debates of 1858* (Chicago, 1958), 65; Utica (N.Y.) *Morning Herald*, June 27, 1860, quoted in Charles M. Segal, ed., *Conversations with Lincoln* (New York, 1961), 34.

14. Speech at Cincinnati, Ohio, September 17, 1859, in *Collected Works*, III, 441–42.

the South. There was no necessity for him to consider Southern positions and viewpoints; it was Douglas who stood in the way, not the South. Lincoln's contest with Douglas was a political contest, to be decided by political arguments and strategies, which in turn determined the extent to which he would carry his attacks on slavery. No holds were barred, for the stakes were high. With Douglas defeated, and the South beaten, Lincoln told his followers, the agitation over the slavery issue would also come to an end. With a Republican ascendancy—which always assumed his own political ascendancy—domestic harmony and sectional peace would once more prevail, and the future of the republic would be secured.

1

The Politics of Slavery

"I have always hated slavery," Lincoln declared in 1858, "I think as much as any Abolitionist." That he had always disliked slavery, argued occasionally for its restriction, and assumed that it would eventually go away, is beyond argument. Countless Americans, Southerners (even slaveholders) as well as Northerners, felt the same way. But that he had always opposed slavery with the zeal and fervor of the abolitionists was much less certain. Lincoln paid little attention to the institution before 1854, and made no effort to conceal the fact. He had, he confessed, "always been quiet about it" because he thought that "everybody was against it." For over two decades, from the beginning of his political career to the passage of the Kansas-Nebraska Act, slavery had been a "minor question" for Lincoln, even though it had fomented some of the most volatile party and sectional battles in Congress during the 1830s and 1840s.[1]

Many of those who have studied and written on Lincoln, however, would have it otherwise. Anxious to establish his credentials as a lifelong crusader against slavery, they have searched his early life for evidence of a strong antislavery position. For example, they

1. Speech at Chicago, Illinois, July 10, 1858, Speech at Springfield, Illinois, July 17, 1858, in *The Collected Works of Abraham Lincoln*, ed. Roy P. Basler et al. (9 vols.; New Brunswick, N.J., 1954), II, 492, 514. Lincoln dismissed the battles in Congress as simply "an occasional brush" with slavery. Speech at Princeton, Illinois, July 4, 1856, in *Collected Works*, II, 346.

have seized upon a protest lodged by Lincoln in 1837, when he was a young Illinois legislator, against resolutions passed by the legislature that dealt with the subject of slavery. The protest, now widely regarded as a protest against slavery, maintained that slavery was "founded on both injustice and bad policy," a mild enough statement that carefully skirted the moral question. Yet Lincoln went on to insist that the "promulgation of abolition doctrines" tended to increase rather than abate slavery's evils. The statement was made in the midst of the abolition petition controversy, when abolitionists flooded Congress with memorials and petitions asking that slavery be abolished in the states and the District of Columbia. Congress' adoption of the famous "gag" rule the year before had only exacerbated the controversy. Lincoln, and a fellow member who also signed the document, gave the abolitionists little comfort, for they denied that Congress possessed the constitutional power to interfere with slavery in the states and, while agreeing that Congress did have the power to abolish slavery in the District, they argued that it ought not exercise it without the consent of the people who lived there. Neither argument was acceptable to the abolition movement. It seems clear that Lincoln was protesting against the new militancy of the abolitionists more than he was objecting to slavery.[2]

From the moment Lincoln first entered political life as a candidate for the state legislature during the decisive 1832 presidential election, he had demonstrated an unswerving fidelity to the party of Henry Clay and to Clay's American System, the program of internal improvements, protective tariff, and centralized banking that to Lincoln held the key to America's future growth and development. As a Whig, he had proved to be a talented party organizer and political operator who was thoroughly attuned to the intense partisanship that characterized the Jackson era. He directed his skill and energy toward the maintenance of party discipline and regularity, and reacted indignantly against those issues that threatened to sow discord within the party ranks. The slavery question, thrust into polit-

2. Protest in Illinois Legislature on Slavery, March 3, 1837, in *Collected Works*, I, 74–75. For background to the protest, see Albert J. Beveridge, *Abraham Lincoln, 1809–1858* (2 vols.; Boston, 1928), I, 188–95. In 1860, Lincoln recalled that the protest had defined his position on slavery, and that "so far as it goes, it was then the same that it is now." Autobiography Written for John L. Scripps, June, 1860, in *Collected Works*, IV, 65.

ical discourse by the abolition movement, aroused Lincoln's fears that a separate antislavery party might weaken Whig strength if it were not met with some form of political accommodation.[3]

Rejecting abolition doctrines for himself, Lincoln nonetheless sought antislavery support without committing either himself or his party to an antislavery position. Following the presidential election of 1840, he credited the abolitionists with having helped to elect William Henry Harrison. "Not that we fell into abolition doctrines," he explained, "but that we took up a man whose position induced them to join us in his election." The tactic was less successful four years later, when the Liberty party drew off enough Whig votes in New York to give the state, and the election, to James K. Polk. Lincoln was outraged. Directing his anger at the abolitionists, he denounced their hypocrisy in the "most scathing language." While they professed "great horror" at the annexation of Texas and the extension of slavery, he charged, they had helped to achieve those very measures by allowing the Democrats to win the election. It was not the Texas issue that bothered Lincoln, for he admitted that he "never could very clearly see how the annexation would augment the evil of slavery," but rather it was the perfidy of antislavery Whigs in abandoning their party's candidate. The country's dramatic territorial expansion did not excite Lincoln; on the contrary, he rejected notions of manifest destiny and ridiculed the pretensions of Young America. Of far greater concern was the task of preserving Whig party unity in the face of the divisive issues raised by expansion.[4]

Although Lincoln had asserted that he "never was much interested in the Texas question," it was the annexation issue that elicited one of his first reasoned responses to the issue of slavery and slavery extension. "I hold it to be a paramount duty of us in the free states," he wrote privately in 1845, "due to the Union of the states, and perhaps to liberty itself (paradox though it may seem) to let the slav-

3. For Lincoln's role as a Whig ideologue and manager, see Joel H. Silbey, "'Always a Whig in Politics': The Partisan Life of Abraham Lincoln," *Papers of the Abraham Lincoln Association*, VIII (1986), 22; and Daniel Walker Howe, "Abraham Lincoln and the Transformation of Northern Whiggery," in Howe, *The Political Culture of the American Whigs* (Chicago, 1979), 263–98.

4. Lincoln to Usher F. Linder, March 22, 1848, Lincoln to Williamson Durley, October 3, 1845, Speech at Lacon, Illinois, November 1, 1848, in *Collected Works*, I, 458, 347–48, II, 14.

ery of the other states alone; while, on the other hand, I hold it to be equally clear, that we should never knowingly lend ourselves directly or indirectly, to prevent that slavery from dying a natural death—to find new places for it to live in, when it can no longer exist in the old." The operative phrase is the last one: only when slavery could no longer exist in the "old places," that is, in the slave-holding states, could its restriction be justified. Obviously, that was not the situation in 1845. If slaves should be taken into Texas, Lincoln stated, "there would be just so many the fewer left, where they were taken from." Lincoln did not view the annexation issue as a threat to freedom.[5]

Lincoln also rejected the view of the antislavery radicals that the Mexican War had its origin in a conspiracy to extend slavery. As a member of Congress during the war's last stage, he attacked President Polk for overstepping the constitutional bounds of presidential power and charged him with having deliberately deceived the people in his eagerness to provoke a conflict with Mexico. Although many writers have perpetuated the myth that Lincoln's attacks were motivated by the slavery issue, Lincoln carefully separated himself from those who believed that the war "originated for the purpose of extending slave territory." And he bristled when his condemnation of the president was confused with an opposition to the war itself, for as he pointed out over and over again, he had never hesitated to support needed measures for men and supplies. Once the war had begun, he felt, it was the duty of all "good citizens and patriots" to support it, a position that was shared by many Whigs. Lincoln agreed, moreover, that the United States should take territory from Mexico, but he was never sure how much, stipulating only that the acquisition should not go so far to the south "as to enlarge and agrivate [sic] the distracting question of slavery."[6]

5. Lincoln to Williamson Durley, October 3, 1845, in *Collected Works*, I, 347–48.
6. Speech at Wilmington, Delaware, June 10, Lincoln to Linder, March 22, Speech in the House of Representatives on the War with Mexico, January 12, Fragment on What General Taylor Ought to Say, March, 1848, in *Collected Works*, I, 476, 457, 432, 454. For more on Lincoln's position on the Mexican War, see G. S. Boritt, "A Question of Political Suicide: Lincoln's Opposition to the Mexican War," *Journal of the Illinois State Historical Society*, LXVII (February, 1974), 79–100; and Mark E. Neely, Jr., "Lincoln and the Mexican War: An Argument by Analogy," *Civil War History*, XXIV (March, 1978), 5–24.

If Lincoln did not connect the Mexican War with slavery, there were many who did. In Congress, between late 1847 and 1849, he witnessed some of the most acrimonious debates over slavery since the Missouri Compromise was approved over twenty-five years before, but he took no part in them. The "most conspicuous feature of Congressman Lincoln's course with reference to slavery," the historian of his congressional term has written, was "his discreet silence." He voted to receive antislavery petitions, and even offered one himself, but appeared to be moved more by John Quincy Adams' eloquent defense of the right of petition than by their substance; and he supported compensated emancipation in the District of Columbia provided (as he had insisted in 1837) it was first approved by a referendum of free white male citizens, a condition that was angrily rejected by the abolitionists. Lincoln voted for the Wilmot Proviso, which would bar slavery from the territory acquired from Mexico, not forty times as he would later boast, but more like five times. He later told his constituents that he would have withdrawn his support of the Wilmot Proviso if he thought the measure might endanger the Union. Like most Northern Whigs, he opposed with his votes if not verbally the extension of slavery into the newly acquired lands. "I am a Northern man, or rather, a Western free state man," he explained, "with a constituency I believe to be, and with personal feelings I know to be, against the extension of slavery."[7]

Lincoln returned to the stump in the 1848 presidential campaign, and as he had in the two previous national contests, he fought to keep antislavery Whigs from defecting to a third party, in this instance the Free Soil party. The Whig party, he told New England abolitionists, was the only "true . . . free soil organization," even though it had nominated a Louisiana slaveholder, Zachary Taylor, to the top of its ticket. Everyone agreed that slavery was an evil, he observed, but there was nothing that could be done about it in those states "where we do not live." On the issue of slavery's expansion,

7. Donald W. Riddle, *Congressman Abraham Lincoln* (Urbana, 1957), 162–79; Remarks and Resolution Concerning Abolition of Slavery in the District of Columbia, January 10, 1849, Speech in the House of Representatives on the Presidential Question, July 27, 1848, in *Collected Works*, II, 20–22, I, 505; Lincoln, quoted in Mark E. Neely, Jr., "Lincoln's Theory of Representation: A Significant New Lincoln Document," *Lincoln Lore*, No. 1683 (May, 1978), 2.

he claimed that the Whigs were as much opposed as the Van Buren, or Free Soil, party. To some antislavery enthusiasts, however, Lincoln's words lacked the conviction they looked for. His appeal sounded too much like politics as usual. The slavery issue, one reporter suggested, would never be resolved until "old party lines are broken down" and until individuals were willing to sacrifice their attachment to "minor questions and make opposition to slavery the leading idea." Lincoln was unwilling to accept either eventuality. Although his personal feelings were opposed to the institution's extension, he was not ready to make that opposition "the leading idea" in his political feelings. Slavery, as he had said, was still only a "distracting question."[8]

Zachary Taylor was elected, but Lincoln's satisfaction was dimmed when he failed to secure the appointment in the new administration he felt he deserved. He was deeply disappointed that his political excursion outside his own state had not brought him the recognition among Whigs he had sought. His assaults on President Polk, in which he had invested so much hope and energy, had caused scarcely a ripple either in Washington or at home. Politics seemed to lose some of its attraction and its excitement, and he turned away to pursue his law practice, as he later put it, "more assiduously than ever before." National issues and events slipped into the background. He was barely stirred by the bitter controversies leading up to the Compromise of 1850, and when he was suggested as a candidate for Congress that year, he made it clear that he was not interested.

Lincoln's withdrawal, however, was never complete. He was too much the ambitious politician to relish an early retirement. Rather, the years following his departure from Congress became a time for waiting and watching, an opportunity to take stock of his situation, and a chance to calculate his future. His decision was made easier (indeed, it was rendered necessary) by the condition of his party. The Whig organization was in decline. Disagreement within its ranks over the Mexican War and the question of slavery in the new

8. Speech at Boston, Massachusetts, September 15, 1848, Speech at Lowell, Massachusetts, September 16, 1848, Speech at Worcester, Massachusetts, September 12, 1848, Speech at Taunton, Massachusetts, September 21, 1848, in *Collected Works*, II, 5, 6, 3, 9.

territories had taken its toll. The passage of the compromise measures in 1850 only deepened the split. The party had become (as one historian has remarked) both "aimless and anemic."[9]

In 1852, Lincoln served on Winfield Scott's electoral ticket, and as he later recalled, he "did something in the way of canvassing" for the Whig presidential candidate, though on a much reduced scale "owing to the hopelessness of the cause in Illinois." The party's troubles mounted when Henry Clay died during the campaign, to be followed soon afterward by Daniel Webster, leaving a void in the party's upper ranks. Charges of abolitionism hurled against Scott so aggravated the tensions within the party that large numbers of Southern Whigs defected before election day. When Scott was buried by a Democratic landslide, the party seemed beyond repair and many Whigs were ready to pronounce its obituary.

Not so Abraham Lincoln. Still active in the management of local party affairs, he was not prepared to concede that it was no longer a viable political organization. There were aspects of the 1852 campaign, moreover, that gave him hope and a sense of opportunity. While the party had virtually lost its Southern wing, it had increased its strength among free soilers in several Northern states. The Free Soil party, Lincoln declared in one of his few campaign addresses, had broken up, Van Buren had returned to "Locofocoism," and his 120,000 votes were the stakes for which the parties vied. While repelling the charges of abolitionism, Lincoln courted the free soilers (as he had done in earlier campaigns), with some success. Not only did Scott receive more votes in Illinois (while being swamped nationally) than Taylor had received four years before, but the Whigs also elected four congressmen, three more than they had had before. The new congressmen owed their victories to a favorable redistricting of the state and to the free soil vote in the state's northern counties.

The 1852 campaign also marked the beginning of an electioneering technique that would serve Lincoln well in future years. He said little about Winfield Scott, for Scott's cause was hopeless; instead, he concentrated on criticism of Stephen A. Douglas. It was like old

9. Lincoln to Jesse W. Fell, Enclosing Autobiography, December 20, 1859, to the Editors of the *Illinois Journal*, June 5, 1850, in *Collected Works*, III, 512, II, 79; Don E. Fehrenbacher, *Prelude to Greatness: Lincoln in the 1850's* (Stanford, 1962), 26.

times, he remarked, when Douglas "was not so much greater . . . than all the rest of us." Douglas' role in national affairs had changed remarkably since the last presidential election. A principal figure in the passage of the Compromise of 1850 and an active, if unsuccessful, candidate for the Democratic nomination in 1852, Douglas had become the acknowledged leader of the national Democracy. By responding to Douglas' arguments on behalf of Franklin Pierce and by defending the Whig party against his charges, Lincoln knew his own reputation would be benefited.[10]

The death of Henry Clay only a short time after Scott's nomination was a severe loss to both the party and to Lincoln. For the latter, it proved to be an opportunity as well. Clay had always been Lincoln's "beau ideal of a statesman," the fount from which his own political views flowed, and the "great parent of Whig principles." "During my whole political life," Lincoln wrote, "I have loved and revered [him] as a teacher and leader." On July 6, 1852, just a few days after the news of Clay's death reached Springfield, he eulogized the great Kentuckian in what was perhaps his most eloquent statement to that time. Often overlooked by Lincoln's biographers, the eulogy was also one of his most important political statements. The Whig campaign was just getting under way. Lincoln had presided over a planning session of local Whigs just before, and on the day following the eulogy, the Whig state convention met to nominate candidates for state offices and to endorse Scott's candidacy for president. Politics was much on Lincoln's mind; indeed, the Clay eulogy may be viewed as a first address in the 1852 campaign.[11]

Before an audience swelled by a number of Whigs who had trav-

10. Autobiography Written for John L. Scripps, June, 1860, Speech to the Springfield Scott Club, August 14, 26, 1852, in *Collected Works*, IV, 67, II, 156, 136; Arthur Charles Cole, *The Era of the Civil War, 1848–1870*, Sesquicentennial History of Illinois Series, III (1919; rpr. Urbana, 1987), 109–11. Lincoln apparently was appointed to the National Whig Committee during the 1852 campaign, as the Illinois member, but there is no evidence that he served. Beveridge, *Abraham Lincoln*, II, 150. For a close analysis of the Whig party's troubles, see David M. Potter, *The Impending Crisis, 1848–1861*, completed and edited by Don E. Fehrenbacher (New York, 1976), 232–41.

11. First Debate with Stephen A. Douglas at Ottawa, Illinois, August 21, 1858, Speech at Taunton, Massachusetts, September 21, 1848, Lincoln to Daniel Ullmann, February 1, 1861, in *Collected Works*, III, 29, II, 7, IV, 184.

eled to the capital for the state convention, Lincoln reviewed Clay's career and his place in American history in sensitive, adulatory tones, but it was Clay's stand on the "great political questions of his country for the last half century" that provided the real substance of Lincoln's remarks. As he spoke it became clear that in defining Clay's position, Lincoln was in fact describing his own.

Clay's "predominant sentiment," the theme that tied all his statements together, Lincoln declared, was his "deep devotion to the cause of human liberty," his "strong sympathy with the oppressed every where," and his "ardent wish for their elevation." Although a slaveholder, Clay was opposed to slavery "on principle and in feeling," and could not "perceive, that on a question of human right, the negroes were to be excepted from the human race." Yet, Lincoln continued, Clay also recognized that "slavery was already wide spread and deeply seated." It could not be abolished "at *once* . . . without producing a greater evil, even to the cause of human liberty itself." Echoing sentiments he had expressed in the legislature fifteen years before, Lincoln castigated the abolitionists "who would shiver into fragments the Union of these States; tear to tatters its now venerated constitution; and even burn the last copy of the Bible, rather than slavery should continue a single hour." Slavery had become an "unfortunate source of discord," yet Clay had followed the only practical and patriotic course. "No one was so habitually careful to avoid all sectional ground," Lincoln exclaimed. "Whatever he did, he did for the whole country." Clay had rejected both extremes, the abolitionists on the one side and on the other those "few, but an increasing number of men" who would perpetuate slavery by attacking the "white-man's charter of freedom—the declaration that 'all men are created free and equal.'" (There seemed little doubt in Lincoln's mind which of the two groups constituted the greater immediate danger to the republic.)

The significance of the eulogy to Lincoln's political career, as well as to his stand on slavery, is clear. Expressed during a presidential election campaign, at a time when both Whigs and Democrats had endorsed the "finality" of the Compromise of 1850, it was Lincoln's announcement that Clay's middle-of-the-road, pragmatic position was also his own—opposition to slavery in principle, toleration of it in practice, and a vigorous hostility toward the abolition movement. "I can express all my views on the slavery question," he observed, "by quotations from Henry Clay."

But the eulogy also had wider implications, for it not only revealed that Lincoln shared Clay's position on slavery—it also revealed Lincoln's ambition to assume Clay's leadership position in the Whig party. Lincoln perceived himself as a likely successor to the great "Harry of the West." The party, he felt, required some new and fresh leader, a "Western free state man" like himself, if its decline were to be checked. That Lincoln, unlike other eulogists, should have focused on Clay's views on liberty, slavery, and abolitionism was no chance circumstance, for it suggested that he was reaching for a platform upon which all Whigs, North and South, might unite, one that would still the dissension over what he called "that unfortunate source of discord—negro slavery." It was a tall order for a man who had decided not long before to give up an active political life, even if only temporarily, but Lincoln was a man of skill, inner strength, and self-confidence sufficient to carry it off. He worked, moreover, from a firm and stable political base, in a state that had ties to both North and South. All he needed was some new catalyst, some critical moment that in its urgency would overcome the differences within his party.[12]

That moment was provided by Stephen A. Douglas. The passage by Congress of Douglas' Kansas-Nebraska Act in the spring of 1854 was arguably the most significant event in Lincoln's prewar political career. He was aroused, he recalled six years later, "as he had never been before." It was tantamount to a conversion experience, for he re-entered public life with all the vigor and righteous conviction of a born-again politician. "Suddenly he had a new purpose and a new chance."[13]

Lincoln's response to Douglas' legislation, played out against a backdrop of politics and partisanship, was a political act, undertaken

12. Eulogy on Henry Clay, July 6, 1852, Speech at Carlinville, Illinois, August 31, 1858, in *Collected Works*, II, 121–32 (quotations, 126, 130), III, 79. On Lincoln's eulogy of Clay, see Mark E. Neely, Jr., "American Nationalism in the Image of Henry Clay: Abraham Lincoln's Eulogy on Henry Clay in Context," *Register of the Kentucky Historical Society*, LXXIII (January, 1975), 31–60.

13. Autobiography Written for John L. Scripps, June, 1860, in *Collected Works*, IV, 67; Fehrenbacher, *Prelude to Greatness*, 21.

in a political context, and directed toward certain immediate political goals. Deeply disturbed by slavery's potentially destructive impact upon the stability of the party system, he set out to inject new life into both his dying party and his political career by redefining Henry Clay's antislavery position into a strong new platform for combating Douglas and the Democratic party. Lincoln was persuaded, moreover, that the "great mass of mankind" (Southerners as well as Northerners) thought slavery to be a "great moral wrong." With the passage of Douglas' bill, the issue had become a "great and durable element of popular action," and no statesman, he believed, could "safely disregard it."

Douglas' final version of the Kansas-Nebraska bill created two territories, Kansas and Nebraska, within the Louisiana Purchase, both lying north of the 1820 Missouri Compromise line that defined the area as forever free. According to the bill, however, the question of slavery in the territories was to be decided by the people who would inhabit them—Douglas' doctrine of popular sovereignty—even though the Compromise had already barred slavery from the region. Douglas hoped to avoid a confrontation with the Missouri Compromise restriction by simply ignoring it, confident that soil, climate, and what he called the "necessary pursuits of people" would effectively discourage the extension of slavery. To his dismay, however, slave-state interests insisted instead on the outright repeal of what was viewed by 1854 as an odious and discriminatory restriction on Southern rights. Douglas reluctantly acquiesced, but predicted that the repeal would "raise a hell of a storm." Indeed it did, as Douglas and his followers almost immediately became the targets in a political controversy that was unprecedented for its bitterness and abusive vilification, a conflict in which Lincoln would ultimately play a principal part.

What Lincoln never acknowledged in his assaults against Douglas and the repeal of the Missouri Compromise restriction was that the initial demand for repeal came not from the Little Giant but from members of Lincoln's own party. The fact must surely have been known to him. Ironically, the first move toward repeal was made by a Whig senator from Kentucky, Archibald Dixon, who not only shared Lincoln's admiration for Henry Clay but who had been elected to fill Clay's seat in the Senate. There is further evidence to suggest that William H. Seward, senator from New York and leader of the Northern Whigs, quietly encouraged Southern members of the party in their demand for repeal on the ground that it would render Douglas' bill more objectionable and thus easier to defeat.[14]

The reactions in the North to the repeal of the Missouri Compromise are well known. Abolitionists, free soilers, and antislavery persons of all stripes joined in a chorus of vituperation against Douglas and his Democratic supporters. Douglas was charged with perpetrating a "gross violation of a sacred pledge" and a "bold scheme against American liberty," and with being a participant in an "atrocious plot" to convert the new territories "into a dreary region of despotism, inhabited by masters and slaves." Mass meetings and rallies protested the legislation and called for action to meet the threat of slavery expansion. Party lines were thrown into confusion amid demands for a new political organization that would resist the aggressions of Douglas and the Slave Power.

Reactions in Illinois were no less volatile. "We were thunderstruck and stunned," Lincoln observed, "and we reeled and fell in utter confusion." Whigs united in opposition to the repeal, while defections from the Democratic ranks eroded Douglas' strength in his own state. Speakers from outside Illinois—Kentucky's abolitionist Cassius M. Clay, Ohio congressman Joshua R. Giddings, and Salmon P. Chase—traversed the state bent on discrediting Douglas among his constituents. Abolitionists like Chicago's Ichabod Codding and Congressman Owen Lovejoy emerged to add their voices to the protests.

The *Illinois State Journal*, the Whig party's official organ in the state capital for which Lincoln often wrote editorials, joined the barrage and fired its salvos against Douglas. The Kansas-Nebraska Act, the paper declared, was a desperate demagogue's desperate measure "to accomplish ambitious ends." Reflecting the direction of Lincoln's political strategy, the paper carefully absolved Southerners of any

14. Speech at Peoria, Illinois, October 16, 1854, in *Collected Works*, II, 281–82; Robert W. Johannsen, *Stephen A. Douglas* (New York, 1973), 404 (for the development of the Kansas-Nebraska Act in its several versions, see 405–18); Mrs. Archibald Dixon, *The True History of the Missouri Compromise and Its Repeal* (Cincinnati, 1899), 438–45; Archibald Dixon to the Editor of the Louisville *Times*, January 28, 1854, reprinted in the Washington *National Intelligencer*, January 30, 1854; Glyndon G. Van Deusen, *William Henry Seward* (New York, 1967), 150, 586–87.

complicity in the repeal of the Missouri Compromise. Southerners, the editor pointed out, understood the "mischief of slavery" and "deplored it as an evil" (where Douglas presumably did not), and favored its extension only in order to maintain their "proportionate balance" in the national government. Echoing Lincoln's fear of the destabilizing influence of abolitionism, the paper expressed concern that Douglas' bill would release a torrent of "abolition fanaticism" on the land, disrupting the party system and leading to the formation of geographical parties that would ultimately endanger the Union itself—a fairly accurate prediction of what actually did happen. At the same time, it bowed, as Lincoln also would, to Northern fears that a massive slave migration would soon engulf the new territories, predicting that thousands of slaves would enter Kansas within a few months and that slaveholders would use them as "squatters" to claim all the good land in the territory. The paper's position, the editor assured his readers, sprang from "no ill feelings toward the south, or the democratic party, nor from any sympathy with abolitionists." Its purpose was simply "to keep slavery on its own ground."[15]

As the protests raged and the controversy swirled around him, Lincoln bided his time. If he was aroused as never before, he did not reveal the fact until eight months after the Kansas-Nebraska bill had been introduced and three months after it had passed. By that time virtually all the arguments against the legislation had been voiced; when Lincoln finally made his move, it was almost anticlimactic. He waited until Congress had adjourned and the state's congressional delegation had returned from Washington, and then deliberately calculated his re-entry into state politics to coincide with the fall election campaign. His goal, he said, was to secure the re-election of Richard Yates, the Whig congressman from the Springfield district; of secondary importance was his own candidacy for a seat in the state legislature, a move he took only because he thought it would aid Yates. He insisted that he had "no broader aim or object" than to see Yates returned to the House of Representatives, but it soon became clear that he had higher stakes in mind.

15. Johannsen, *Stephen A. Douglas*, 418–19, 447–56; Speech at Peoria, Illinois, October 16, 1854, in *Collected Works*, II, 282; Springfield *Illinois State Journal*, January 13, March 18, January 21, June 13, 24, April 3, 1854.

A United States senator would be chosen at the next legislative session. Because the incumbent, James Shields (with whom Lincoln had almost fought a duel in earlier years), was a loyal friend and supporter of Stephen A. Douglas, Lincoln expected the election to attract considerable national attention as a test of Douglas' strength on his home ground. He also believed that the furor over the Kansas-Nebraska Act could be made to work to the advantage of the Whigs, reviving their party and enabling them not only to take control of the legislature but also to elect a Whig to the United States Senate. Most important of all, Lincoln was determined to be that new senator. It was his "grand opportunity," recalled his law partner, and he seized it and rode "to glory on the popular waves." [16]

Lincoln prepared for his campaign with an "uncommon thoroughness." During the months following the passage of Douglas' bill, when he was not arguing law cases, he was seen "nosing" about in the state library, studying the debates in Congress, reviewing the protests of antislavery leaders, and "pumping his brains and his imagination" for arguments with which to demolish the Little Giant. It was serious business, for nothing mattered more to Lincoln than that political opinion in the state be mobilized against Douglas and that it be drawn to the side of the Whig party. "You know how anxious I am," he wrote his friend John M. Palmer, "that this Nebraska measure shall be rebuked and condemned every where." [17]

16. Autobiography Written for John L. Scripps, June, 1860, Lincoln to Elihu N. Powell, November 27, 1854, in *Collected Works*, IV, 67, II, 289; Horace White to Lincoln, October 25, 1854, Richard Yates to Lincoln, December 22, 1854, in David C. Mearns, ed., *The Lincoln Papers* (2 vols.; Garden City, N.Y., 1948), I, 190, 198; William H. Herndon to Jesse W. Weik, February 11, 1887, in Emanuel Hertz, *The Hidden Lincoln: From the Letters and Papers of William H. Herndon* (New York, 1938), 173.

17. Beveridge, *Abraham Lincoln*, II, 238; Springfield *Illinois State Register*, October 6, 1854; Lincoln to John M. Palmer, September 7, 1854, in *Collected Works*, II, 228. In his letter to Palmer, a popular Democrat and member of the state senate who broke with Douglas over the Kansas-Nebraska Act, Lincoln suggested somewhat disingenuously that he would not have entered the campaign if Palmer had been the Democratic nominee for Yates's congressional seat. "I still should have voted for the whig candidate," he wrote, "but I should have made no speeches, written no letters; and you would have been elected by at least a thousand majority." Palmer's election by itself, Lincoln observed, would be a sufficient and satisfactory rebuke of Douglas' bill. Furthermore, he appealed to Palmer not to support the Douglas candidate lest

Two days after Douglas returned to Illinois from Washington, Lincoln opened his campaign. Although speaking ostensibly for Yates, it was Douglas he had been waiting for, cognizant of the benefits to be derived from confronting the Democratic leader directly. Six of his ten reported speeches were delivered outside Yates's congressional district, lending credence to the suggestion that he had something more than Yates's re-election in mind. At several locations, Lincoln and Douglas listened to one another and shared the same audiences. Lincoln's arguments, delivered with varying degrees of emphasis, followed the same general themes on each occasion, but one of the speeches stood out above all the rest as his model. Although he had delivered it earlier at Springfield, the state capital, it was Lincoln's address at Peoria on October 16, 1854, that he carefully wrote out for the press, the only one for which there is a verbatim report. Thus, the Peoria Speech, as it is now known in the Lincoln canon, became the inaugural statement in Lincoln's reactivated career.[18]

At age forty-five, Lincoln delivered his first significant discourse on the slavery issue. There was little that was original in his arguments, for behind him he had eight months of bitter and relentless attacks against the Kansas-Nebraska Act and its authors by some of the nation's leading antislavery spokesmen. He had done his homework well, borrowing heavily from the statements of men like Ohio's abolitionist Salmon P. Chase and adapting them to his own particular ends. Indeed, the position he developed followed the same general lines of argument found in the familiar free soil posi-

---

his anti-Nebraska friends follow his example. One may assume that Lincoln, with the senatorial election in the offing, knew the importance of building a bridge to the anti-Nebraska Democrats. Palmer was running for re-election to the legislature, "only remotely influenced . . . by hostility to slavery," as he later recalled, but "chiefly concerned by the fact that the repeal of the Missouri Compromise reopened the slavery agitation." *Personal Recollections of John M. Palmer: The Story of an Earnest Life* (Cincinnati, 1901), 68.

18. Douglas' speaking engagements carried him through northern and central Illinois, in those districts where Democratic candidates were most likely to have trouble. In Bloomington, Douglas and Lincoln met in the former's hotel room to discuss their speaking arrangements, where Douglas declined Lincoln's invitation to meet in a joint debate. Johannsen, *Stephen A. Douglas*, 453–58. Lincoln's Peoria Speech was printed in seven issues of the *Illinois State Journal*, October 21, 23, 24, 25, 26, 27, 28, 1854.

tion that had evolved since the early 1840s. At the same time, as Douglas reminded him and Lincoln conceded, his views—especially his insistence on respect for the constitutional rights of the slave states—differed from those held by others who opposed the Kansas-Nebraska legislation.[19]

Writers and scholars over the years have elevated the Peoria Speech to the level of infallible truth, viewing it as a statement of moral indignation and urgency against slavery, as a lofty and eloquent appeal to restore the ideals of the Founding Fathers, and as one of the imperishable speeches of all time. With proper allowance for the excessive adulation and hyperbole identified with all things Lincoln, one may find suggestions of these in his words. What is usually overlooked, however, is the speech's unmistakable political character and purpose. It provided Lincoln with a foundation upon which he built an antislavery career that eventually carried him to political heights he did not even dream of in 1854. He would quote from it extensively and often during the next six years, and as late as the eve of the 1860 election he would still insist (although less than persuasively) that his ideas had not changed since he first defined them at Peoria.

Lincoln's purpose was to point out the wrong of Douglas' repeal of the Missouri Compromise and to call vigorously for its restoration. He undertook his task with all the warmth and skill of a seasoned politician, in a manner commensurate with the ability of his opponent. Douglas' oratorical power was almost legendary: "He is the grand master of human passion," observed the editor of Springfield's official Whig paper, "and rules the crowd with an iron rule, because he governs them by and through their passions." In Lincoln, the Little Giant met his match. Lincoln denied any intention of answering Douglas' arguments, or of assailing his motives, then proceeded to do both, hurling "hot bolts of truth" that according to William Herndon utterly demolished the senator. No holds were barred as Lincoln employed all the tactics familiar to rough-and-tumble mid-nineteenth-century political discourse—exaggeration, deliberate misrepresentation, false analogy—and spiced his attacks

19. Speech at Peoria, Illinois, October 16, 1854, in *Collected Works*, II, 282.

with what were known as "Lincolnisms," the jokes and funny stories with which he ridiculed his opponents' views.[20]

Lincoln offered a detailed historical chronology to prove that the Missouri Compromise had been a sacred and inviolable compact between the sections; and he closely examined the original intent of the Founding Fathers to show that the restriction of slavery was embedded in the very foundations of the republic. It was against these fundamental propositions that Douglas had arrayed himself when he repealed the Missouri Compromise. In language suggestive of the radical abolitionists, Lincoln charged that the terms of the Kansas-Nebraska Act masked Douglas' real intentions—his "covert *real* zeal"—to spread the institution of slavery, imputing motives Douglas was surprised he held. Twice in the speech, Lincoln warned his audience that Douglas and his kind harbored designs that went far beyond the extension of slavery to the territories north of the Missouri Compromise line. Douglas intended to establish a prospective principle—popular sovereignty—that would allow slavery to spread "to every other part of the wide world, where men can be found inclined to take it," a charge Lincoln later developed into a full-fledged conspiracy theory. Douglas' bill, in other words, held within its terms consequences that would not only alter the nature of republican America but that would also affect the entire world.[21]

Lincoln joined the chorus of condemnation against the Kansas-Nebraska Act by singling out Douglas as the sole target for his assaults, as if the Illinois senator had accomplished the repeal of the Missouri Compromise by himself. For the slaveholding South, in whose interest Douglas had allegedly acted, Lincoln had only benign words. Directing his remarks to "Americans south, as well as north," he extended the hand of friendship to Southerners, especially to Southern Whigs, whose support was necessary to the revitalization of the party. "I . . . wish," he said, "to be no less than National in all the positions I take." He carefully distinguished be-

20. Springfield *Illinois State Journal*, October 10, 1854; Speech at Peoria, Illinois, October 16, 1854, in *Collected Works*, II, 248; William H. Herndon and Jesse W. Weik, *Herndon's Life of Lincoln*, ed. Paul M. Angle (Cleveland, 1949), 297; Springfield *Illinois State Register*, October 6, 1854.

21. Speech at Peoria, Illinois, October 16, 1854, in *Collected Works*, II, 255, 273.

tween slavery as it existed in the states on the one hand, and its extension to the territories on the other, lest his statements be misunderstood as an attack upon the South.

Against slavery in the states Lincoln offered no argument except to repeat his dislike of the institution in the abstract. Although he hated the "monstrous injustice" of slavery, he nevertheless tolerated it wherever it existed. In language that echoed his eulogy on Clay, he pointed out that slavery in the states was protected by legal and constitutional guarantees. No matter how objectionable people may think them, these guarantees had to be observed and respected. He agreed with the South that it would be extremely difficult to rid the nation of slavery "in any satisfactory way," short of drastically altering the frame of America's republican government. Lincoln called this the "argument of Necessity," a kind of escape clause he said he derived from the Founding Fathers that justified the distinction between slavery as an existing institution and its extension to free territory. Lincoln made it clear, moreover, that he harbored no ill-feeling toward Southerners because they held slaves. He was not even sure that he would not be a slaveowner if he were in their situation. "I think I would not hold one in slavery," he mused, "yet the point is not clear enough for me to denounce people upon." Southern slaveholders, he suggested, were "just what we would be in their situation."[22]

To Lincoln, the similarities between Northerners and Southerners were more important than their differences. He reminded his audience that people in the North were just as responsible for slavery as those in the South. "When southern people tell us," he declared, that "they are no more responsible for the origin of slavery than we; I acknowledge the fact." He recognized the dilemma which the existence of slavery had thrust upon the South. In their hearts, Lincoln seemed to be saying, Southerners knew slavery to be wrong. They "manifest in many ways, their sense of the wrong of

---

22. *Ibid.*, 276, 248, 255, 274–75. Lincoln returned to his "doctrine of necessity" frequently during later years in order to justify his toleration of slavery's existence while arguing for its "ultimate extinction"; see, for example, Speech at Chicago, Illinois, July 10, 1858, and Speech at Springfield, Illinois, July 17, 1858, in *Collected Works*, II, 501, 520–21. Gerhard E. Mulder has related the "doctrine" to deeper elements in Lincoln's thought in his "Abraham Lincoln and the Doctrine of Necessity," *Lincoln Herald*, LXVI (Summer, 1964), 59–66.

slavery," yet they could not be blamed for not doing what he himself would not know how to do. "If all earthly power were given me," he confessed, "I should not know what to do, as to the existing institution." Like Henry Clay, he believed that the colonization of freed slaves outside the United States was the best course of action, but he realized that it was impractical, if not impossible to achieve.

"What then?" Lincoln asked. To free the slaves and hold them "among us as underlings" would not improve their condition. They might as well remain slaves. To free them and make them "politically and socially our equals" was no less objectionable. His own feelings, he said, would not allow him to accept racial equality, but even if they did, "those of the great mass of white people" would not accept it. "A universal feeling," he added as a corollary to the "doctrine of necessity," whether well- or ill-founded, "can not be safely disregarded." Finally, Lincoln suggested that a program of gradual emancipation might work, but the initiative would have to come from the Southerners themselves. He would not "undertake to judge our brethren of the south" if they should be reluctant to do so.[23]

By focusing on the threat of slavery expansion implied in the repeal of the Missouri Compromise while virtually excusing Southerners for holding slaves in their states, Lincoln was able to place his argument on the broad spectrum of Whig thought and to be, as he said, truly national in his position. The mixed nature of Illinois' population demanded no less, for he knew that his appeal would have to be acceptable to voters of both Southern and Northern backgrounds if he were to succeed in saving the Whig party. But while Lincoln credited Southerners with knowing that slavery was wrong, he made no such concession to Douglas. His enemy was Douglas, not the South. To achieve his ends, it was necessary to portray the Little Giant in extreme terms, as representing the proslavery argument in its most insidious form. He accused Douglas of proclaiming a moral right to own slaves, and of seeking the extension of slavery throughout the land, if not the world. For the first time, Douglas had revealed his vulnerability, his power was eroding, and his hold

23. Speech at Peoria, Illinois, October 16, 1854, in *Collected Works*, II, 254–56.

on the state's politics was weakened. Lincoln was determined to make the most of it.

He rejected as a *"lullaby"* argument Douglas' assurances that slavery could not profitably exist in the two new territories of Kansas and Nebraska, and that if allowed to make the decision for themselves, the settlers were more likely to prohibit slavery than to legalize it. Although Lincoln later admitted that slaveowners had not exactly poured into the region south of the Missouri Compromise and west of Arkansas, or into Utah and New Mexico territories where popular sovereignty also applied, he feared the worst for Kansas and Nebraska. In any case, he exclaimed, Douglas' doctrine of territorial self-government had no "just application" to those territories, presumably because the "negro *is* a man" and therefore could not be a slave.

When Lincoln addressed Douglas' doctrine of popular sovereignty, he transformed a simple, straightforward, and pragmatic proposition into something complicated and even sinister. If the Negro was a man, as Lincoln said everyone, even Southerners, conceded, then it was a "total destruction of self-government" to hold him as a slave in the territories. Extending his critique into a commentary on governance that seemed to belie his own Whig orientation, Lincoln argued that "no man is good enough to govern another man, *without the other's consent.*" It was the "leading principle" of American republicanism, deriving its legitimacy from the injunctions in the Declaration of Independence that "all men are created equal" and that governments derive their just powers from the consent of the governed. Just how far he would carry what he called "this ancient faith" was revealed when he insisted: "Allow ALL the governed an equal voice in the government, and that, and that only is self-government." [24]

What did Lincoln mean? Was he proposing an absolute universal

24. *Ibid.*, 262, 265–66. Lincoln's perception of popular sovereignty was much narrower than that of Douglas. "The doctrine of self-government," he commented, "is right—absolutely and eternally right," but he argued that it could not be extended to the question of slavery. Lincoln was either unfamiliar with or he deemed irrelevant the tradition of Western protest against the restrictions of the territorial system; Douglas had been sensitive to the protests and had sought to "liberalize" the system in his territorial bills, including the Kansas-Nebraska Act. See Robert W. Johannsen, *The Frontier, the Union, and Stephen A. Douglas* (Urbana, 1989), chaps. 1, 2, and 6.

suffrage, a suffrage without restriction? It was a startling statement for mid-nineteenth-century Americans, and his listeners must have reacted with surprise. However, Lincoln allowed them no time to ponder his meaning for he added, literally in the next breath, that he must not be understood as "contending for the establishment of political and social equality between the whites and blacks." Reminding his audience that blacks "are already amongst us," Lincoln invoked his "doctrine of necessity" once again. He had been speaking only in abstract terms and did not intend his statements to have a practical application. As if to allay any anxieties the members of his audience might have, he assured them that the "whole nation" was concerned that the "best use" be made of the territories. "We want them for the homes of free white people."[25]

Lincoln's rejection of Douglas' popular sovereignty sprang in part from the distrust of the popular will and pessimistic view of human nature that often characterized Whig political theory. While he believed self-government to be "absolutely and eternally right" in an abstract sense, on a more practical level he had no faith that the people in the territories, if given the opportunity, would reject slavery. Self-interest, he contended, would overpower their better judgment, for slavery was "founded in the selfishness of man's nature." Restricting slavery's spread would have the effect of bridling the avarice and corruption that many Americans had warned would ultimately destroy the republic. "In our greedy chase to make profit of the negro," Lincoln cautioned, adding to the racial overtones of his argument, "let us beware, lest we 'cancel and tear to pieces' even the white man's charter of freedom."[26]

Lincoln also denied Douglas' claim that the Kansas-Nebraska Act

25. Speech at Peoria, Illinois, October 16, 1854, in *Collected Works*, II, 268. In arguing that settlement of the territories be restricted to free white people, Lincoln was reflecting a point of view that was commonly held in Illinois and elsewhere in the North. Illinois had a tradition, dating back to its territorial period, of restrictive and exclusionary legislation against blacks, culminating in the 1853 Black Law that barred blacks from residing in the state, the "most severe anti-Negro measure passed by a free state." Eugene H. Berwanger, *The Frontier Against Slavery: Western Anti-Negro Prejudice and the Slavery Extension Controversy* (Urbana, 1967), 49. Although Lincoln had long been active in state politics, he seemed never to question this legislation; nor did he speak out against the Black Law.

26. Speech at Peoria, Illinois, October 16, 1854, in *Collected Works*, II, 265, 271, 276.

was a "great Union-saving measure." On the contrary, he suggested, the repeal of the Missouri Compromise carried with it the total repudiation of that spirit of compromise that had long held the Union together. If the repeal were not overturned, he warned, that spirit will have been "strangled and cast from us forever." In that case, he predicted, extremists in both the North and the South would be emboldened to stir up animosity and hatred between the sections. On the other hand, restore the Missouri Compromise, and the "national faith, national confidence, and the national feeling of brotherhood" would also be restored. The conflict between the sections over the issue of slavery would be stilled, and the spirit that had preserved the Union thus far could be "safely trusted for all the future." However, invoking necessity once again, Lincoln assured his audience, almost as an afterthought, that as much as he hated slavery, he would agree to its extension "rather than see the Union dissolved." [27]

Lincoln's Peoria Speech was as much a call for political action as it was a calculated response to the passage of the Kansas-Nebraska Act. Elect a House of Representatives, he urged the voters, that would reinstate the Missouri Compromise, and choose as United States senators those who had expressed "their will" against Douglas (an appeal with personal as well as partisan relevance). Furthermore, he entreated the people of the South to stand with him and his friends in the North on what he called the "middle ground" between the "dangerous extremes" of the Northern abolitionist and the Southern disunionist. "This," he declared, was the "good old whig ground."

Lincoln's appeal during the election campaigns in the fall of 1854 was not unlike those he had made in earlier campaigns, when he had tried to persuade antislavery Whigs to find accommodation in the national party rather than in sectional third-party movements. In asking Southerners to join him, he pointed out that they would lose nothing they had not already lost thirty-four years before. On the contrary, they had much to gain. By restoring the Missouri Compromise, Lincoln promised, America's "republican robe" would be repurified, washed white in the spirit of the American Revolution.

27. *Ibid.*, 270, 272.

By depriving slavery of the opportunity to expand into the new territories, by turning it back upon its existing legal rights and constitutional protection, the institution would be returned to the "position our fathers gave it." The Declaration of Independence would be readopted.

With rhetoric that soared, he appealed to the deepest patriotic impulses of his audience: "Let north and south—let all Americans—let all lovers of liberty everywhere—join in the great and good work. If we do this, we shall not only have saved the Union; but we shall have so saved it, as to make, and to keep it, forever worthy of the saving. We shall have so saved it," Lincoln concluded with a flourish, "that the succeeding millions of free happy people, the world over, shall rise up, and call us blessed, to the latest generations." [28]

Had central Illinois' voters ever been so stirred? Clearly, Lincoln was directing his remarks beyond the borders of Richard Yates's congressional district. With Stephen A. Douglas in the audience, he no doubt thought—certainly he hoped—that his statements would be given a wide circulation. Although he addressed his remarks southward, it was not likely that his appeal reached a Southern audience. Lincoln's voice was only one of many that were raised against the Kansas-Nebraska Act during that critical year, and there was little to distinguish it from the rest. Douglas had heard it all before; even Lincoln had heard it before when men like Chase, Giddings, and Yates himself had spoken in the state. By the time Lincoln made his move, Southerners had grown weary of the arguments that were cast against the Kansas-Nebraska Act and probably would have been unimpressed with Lincoln's "hot bolts of truth" even if they had been exposed to them. Six months earlier, a writer in the *Southern Literary Messenger* (which Lincoln allegedly read) objected to the "wearisome repetition of the details of the Missouri question, . . . the Declaration of Independence and the ordinance of 1787. . . . These are the stock in trade and in common, the lean larder from which the table must be furnished forth, varying only in the preparation with the talent of the compounder." [29]

28. *Ibid.*, 272, 273, 276.
29. "A Few Thoughts on Slavery," *Southern Literary Messenger*, XX (April, 1854), 193. The Peoria Speech received little or no attention in or outside Illinois during the

After the oratorical heights reached by Lincoln during the campaign, the election results were an anticlimax. Not only were his words not read outside the state, they were also not heeded within. In spite of Lincoln's efforts on his behalf, Richard Yates fell before his Democratic opponent, a friend and loyal supporter of Douglas, and failed to win re-election to the House of Representatives. Lincoln won his race for a seat in the state legislature but was compelled to resign soon after when he learned that he could not be a candidate for the United States Senate while sitting in the electing body. To his chagrin, a Douglas Democrat was elected to fill the vacancy in a special election. Then to top it off, after a couple of months of intensive lobbying among legislators from around the state, Lincoln was passed over in the senatorial election, in favor of Lyman Trumbull, an anti-Nebraska Democrat who had broken with Douglas over the repeal of the Missouri Compromise.

Although personally disappointed, Lincoln found solace in the fact that Douglas and his Act had been rebuked in the statewide returns. An anti-Nebraska majority was elected to the state legislature, and the congressional elections went against the Douglas Democrats by a margin of five to four, suggesting that Lincoln's speeches outside Yates's district were not without effect. "It is a great consolation," Lincoln wrote his friend Elihu Washburne, "to see them worse whipped than I am." [30]

Six weeks after the November elections, in which the Democrats lost ground throughout the North, Douglas wrote with obvious relief but curious shortsightedness, "The Nebraska fight is over." He could not have been more wrong. For Abraham Lincoln, the fight had just begun. He had made his decision and there was no turning back. While he had little hope that the Missouri Compromise would be restored, he was confident that the struggle would continue. Indeed, he was in an advantageous position to see that the struggle *did*

---

following years, until 1860, when it was reprinted in some of Lincoln's campaign biographies. At that time, Southerners read the speech for the first time. One New Orleans editor then commented that Lincoln's words marked him as a "thorough radical Abolitionist" and as such dangerous to the slaveholding states. New Orleans *Daily Crescent*, November 12, 1860, in Dwight L. Dumond, ed., *Southern Editorials on Secession* (New York, 1931), 230.

30. Lincoln to Elihu B. Washburne, February 9, 1855, in *Collected Works*, II, 306.

continue. The groundwork for his resumption of an active political career had been laid. Years later, he recalled that his speeches had "at once attracted a more marked attention than they had ever before done." His position in the politics of his state was secure, and a growing number of Illinoisans now turned to him for leadership and direction. Lincoln had struck just the right chords and had found his issue, the "very thing," one historian has observed, that he "needed and wanted."[31]

31. Douglas to Charles H. Lanphier, December 18, 1854, in Robert W. Johannsen, ed., *The Letters of Stephen A. Douglas* (Urbana, 1961), 331; Autobiography Written for John L. Scripps, June, 1860, in *Collected Works*, IV, 67; Riddle, *Congressman Abraham Lincoln*, 246.

2

The Ultimate Extinction of Slavery

When Congress passed Stephen A. Douglas' Kansas-Nebraska Act and repealed the Missouri Compromise restriction on slavery in the new territories in the spring of 1854, Lincoln recalled, "we believed there was a new era being introduced in the history of the Republic, which tended to the spread and perpetuation of slavery." One may argue whether the threat was as real as Lincoln believed it to be. The fact, however, is unmistakable that if Douglas' Act did not of itself constitute a "new era," the response to it certainly did. The threat, real or not, became an effective political stratagem in the hands of Douglas' rivals. While Lincoln scholars have disagreed over the extent to which Lincoln had actually retired from politics before 1854, there can be no disagreement that the passage of the Kansas-Nebraska Act opened a "new era" in Lincoln's life. It brought vigor to a languishing political career, provided a new platform on which to build his ambitions, offered a fortuitous opportunity to arrest the decline of a political party that seemed to have lost its way, and enabled him to add his voice to the chorus of denunciation that was aimed at Douglas and the power of slavery. The slavery issue was transformed from the "minor question" he said it had always been to him, to (as he put it) "that irresistible power which for fifty years has shaken the government and agitated the people . . . the only serious danger that has threatened our institutions."[1]

For Lincoln, the protests against the Kansas-Nebraska Act that swept the North, threatening to derange the Democratic party, provided the issue that could bring new life and energy to the Whigs, restore the tradition of leadership that had died with Clay and Webster two years before, and prepare the way for a glorious comeback in the presidential election of 1856. Whigs of the North and South, he optimistically believed, might unite on a platform that restored the Missouri Compromise, meeting the demand of Northerners that slavery be restricted from territory that had been free, while acknowledging "fully and fairly" the constitutional and legal protection of slavery in the South, including the slaveholders' right to reclaim their fugitives. While emphasizing the common assumption that slavery was wrong in an abstract sense, he would tolerate it where it had become a practical necessity. The only true Whig ground, he had said, was the middle ground. While arguing that the "spirit of compromise" (of which the Missouri Compromise was the outstanding example) be preserved and protected, Lincoln rejected Douglas' proposition that the people of the territories decide the slavery question for themselves. Because slavery was inherently wrong, it was the responsibility of the national government to prevent its expansion.

Lincoln's position, as developed in his Peoria Speech during the fall election campaign in 1854, was a restatement of a free-soil argument that had been most clearly expressed in Salmon P. Chase's "freedom national doctrine." Stated simply, Chase argued that the "principle of freedom guided national policy and action and that slavery persisted only through local municipal regulations." The Constitution, Chase insisted, granted Congress the power to prohibit the extension of slavery to the national territories while it enjoined the national legislature from interfering with slavery in the states. Chase grounded his doctrine in addition on the equality

1. Second Debate with Stephen A. Douglas at Freeport, Illinois, August 27, 1858, Seventh and Last Debate with Stephen A. Douglas at Alton, Illinois, October 15, 1858, in *The Collected Works of Abraham Lincoln*, ed. Roy P. Basler et al. (9 vols.; New Brunswick, N.J., 1954), III, 71, 310–11.

clause in the Declaration of Independence, "the great fundamental truth, which constitutes the basis of all just government," and on the original intent of the Founding Fathers to limit and discourage slavery, in both instances anticipating Lincoln's declarations against the repeal of the Missouri Compromise.[2]

In Lincoln's hands, Chase's free-soil arguments became a balanced national prescription for restoring the Whig party to its former vitality, a mixture of abstract principle and constitutional reality. But Lincoln also believed that there was more than mere partisan advantage involved, for he was convinced that his position would promote sectional harmony. He saw in his stand the greatest of national missions, one which Whigs in both North and South could proudly undertake—to cleanse and purify the republic and not only save the Union but so save it "as to make and to keep it, forever worthy of the saving."

Lincoln's appeal to the South was more than a rhetorical device, for the South was essential to his plans. Unlike many of the critics of the Kansas-Nebraska Act, he clothed his protests in sympathy for the Southern people, assuring them that he held no prejudice against them because they owned slaves. On the contrary, he appreciated what he described as the Southerners' dilemma—knowing in their hearts that slavery was wrong, but unable, out of necessity, to do anything about it. Like the people in the South, he confessed, he would not know what to do about slavery, even if "all earthly power" were given him. The people of the North, moreover, were just as responsible for slavery as were those of the South. Indeed, they would do no differently if their roles were reversed. Southerners, Lincoln exclaimed, "are just what we would be in their situation. If slavery did not now exist amongst them, they would not introduce it. If it did now exist amongst us, we should not instantly give it up." Slavery, he seemed to be saying, owed its existence not to any

2. Louis S. Gerteis, *Morality & Unity in American Antislavery Reform* (Chapel Hill, 1987), 26, 40–43, 94. Although Chase had expressed this position as early as 1842, he developed it most fully in his senate speech on "Union and Freedom, Without Compromise" on March 26–27, 1850. *Congressional Globe*, 31st Cong., 1st Sess., App., 468–80. The speech was undoubtedly available to Lincoln either through the *Globe* or in its pamphlet edition when he prepared his arguments four years later.

abstract notions of right or wrong but rather to certain peculiar historical circumstances.[3]

Lincoln was not the only Northern Whig who had visions of rebuilding the party on a Missouri Compromise foundation, but he was among the few who persisted in the effort. As a matter of fact, he did not even enter the discussion until long after others had recognized the futility of appealing to the South for help. New York senator William H. Seward and others in Congress hoped that Southern Whigs could be persuaded to support, perhaps even lead, the opposition to the Kansas-Nebraska Act. Their hopes, however, were dashed early in the debates when it became apparent that Southern Whigs would side with the Democrats in support of the repeal of the Missouri Compromise, not because they believed that slaveholders would move to the new territories but because a "wanton insult" to the equality and sovereignty of the slave states had been removed. For many of them, it was a matter of honor. Seward knew, moreover, and Lincoln must have known, that the repeal of the Compromise was not the work of Douglas but of slave-state members of their own party. A disheartened Seward moaned, "We have no longer any bond to Southern Whigs." For the more outspoken antislavery Whigs that was not a bad thing. Some openly rejected any suggestion of an alliance with the South, while one senator rejoiced that "an impassable gulf" had opened between him and Southern members of his party.[4]

Lincoln's emotional and doctrinal attachment to the party of Henry Clay and his stubborn refusal to admit its demise blinded him to the hopelessness of his cause. The only alternative to a united Whig party, he maintained, was the creation of sectional, or geographical, parties, a calamity he wished to avoid. From the beginning of his career, he had been an earnest supporter of the two-party system, believing that in the healthy competition of two strong national organizations lay the strength of the Union itself. In three

3. Speech at Peoria, Illinois, October 16, 1854, in *Collected Works*, II, 273, 276, 255.

4. Frederick W. Seward, *Seward at Washington, as Senator and Secretary of State: A Memoir of His Life, with Selections from His Letters, 1846–1861* (New York, 1891), 217, 219; *Congressional Globe*, 33rd Cong., 1st Sess., App., 764 (Benjamin F. Wade).

earlier presidential elections—1840, 1844, and 1848—he had combated sectional party movements with some limited success. Now, with the conflict between North and South heating up, the national party system was more important than ever. If it should falter, the agitation would be prolonged, bitter hatreds and animosities would be encouraged, and, he feared, the "real knell of the Union" would be sounded.[5]

There were enough straws for him to grasp to inspire his efforts. Both the *Illinois State Journal*, the state's leading Whig paper, and the *National Intelligencer*, the party's national organ (to which Lincoln subscribed), regularly printed reports of Southern opposition to the Kansas-Nebraska Act. "We are glad to see that many Southern papers and Southern Statesmen are taking ground against the disturbance of the Compromise," commented the *Journal*. "The South has now a chance to show its chivalry and honor, and to win back to it the people of the North." Neither side looked forward to another national convulsion over "this vexed question of Slavery," for even the South's most radical paper, the Charleston *Mercury*, predicted that the passage of the Kansas-Nebraska Act would plunge the country into a "wilder crisis" than had ever before been experienced. One New Orleans paper advised Southerners to "stick to all the Compromises" for there would probably be no more. Many rank-and-file Whigs in the South were said to be indifferent toward the repeal of the Missouri Compromise, while others feared a renewal of agitation more than they did the restriction of slavery. Some doubted that the repeal would ever be of practical advantage to the South, agreeing with Douglas that geographic and demographic factors would keep slavery out of the territories in any case.[6]

Southern reactions, as reported in the Whig press, appeared to be mixed, and it was on this that Lincoln apparently placed his hopes. The reports, however, were fragmentary, based as much on wishful

5. Springfield *Illinois State Journal*, June 13, 1854; Speech at Peoria, Illinois, October 16, 1854, in *Collected Works*, II, 272.

6. Springfield *Illinois State Journal*, February 15, April 18, 19, 1854. For Southern Whig reactions to the Kansas-Nebraska Act, see Arthur C. Cole, *The Whig Party in the South* (Washington, D.C., 1913), 298–303; Avery O. Craven, *The Growth of Southern Nationalism, 1848–1861* (Baton Rouge, 1953), 192–203; and William J. Cooper, Jr., *The South and the Politics of Slavery, 1828–1856* (Baton Rouge, 1978), 353–56.

thinking as on fact. Lacking a firsthand acquaintance with the South or with Southern leaders, Lincoln had little opportunity to gauge the nature of Southern thinking (although his reading of the Charleston *Mercury* and the Richmond *Enquirer*, both received in his law office, should have provided some clues). In fact, William J. Cooper has asserted, "no southern party expecting to survive could join with northerners to defeat legislation broadly viewed in the South as recognizing southern honor and establishing southern rights." Even those Southern Whigs who spoke against the Kansas-Nebraska Act nonetheless urged its support, if for no other reason than to demonstrate their soundness on an issue of Southern interest. No matter how they felt about Douglas' Act, Southern Whigs were warned to be suspicious of Northern overtures and were reminded that many Northern Whigs harbored strong antislavery and anti-Southern views. Indeed, so far from responding to Northern appeals, Alexander H. Stephens, Georgia's Whig congressman and a friend of Lincoln, hoped to establish a national party to be led by Southern Whigs, on a platform that endorsed the repeal of the Missouri Compromise. "Hundreds and thousands of Northern Whigs when they see this is our fixed determination," Stephens was confident, "will abandon the Seward ranks of the anti-slavery agitators." Stephens' evaluation of the Whig political scene was no more realistic than was that of Lincoln.[7]

If Lincoln gradually became aware that his strategy had little chance for success among Southern Whigs, he also was dismayed that few Northern antislavery men were willing to endorse his plan to revive the party as the appropriate vehicle for mobilizing free-soil sentiment. The Whig party was in the last stages of collapse and hardly offered an encouraging prospect for maintaining an effective opposition to the expansion of slavery. The party, moreover, was widely perceived as no more resistant to the demands of the Slave Power than the Democratic party. "God help us," exhorted one antislavery editor, "if . . . we have all to admit that the Whig Party is the party of freedom." The party was dying, declared Wendell Phil-

7. Cooper, *The South and the Politics of Slavery*, 355–56, 353; Stephens, quoted in Cole, *Whig Party in the South*, 307. See also Thomas E. Schott, *Alexander H. Stephens of Georgia: A Biography* (Baton Rouge, 1988), 174.

lips, precisely because it had lowered itself to the level of "servile bidding for Southern fellowship."[8]

Similar sentiments were expressed by free soilers and abolitionists in Illinois. Not only were they opposed to affiliation with the Whig party, but they were also reluctant to accept Lincoln as an antislavery leader, in view of his late conversion to the cause. Chicago's militant abolitionist newspaper, the *Free West*, conceded that Lincoln was a "Good Fellow at heart" but strongly advised against supporting him. "He is reported to be a Compromise Whig," the paper charged, correctly, "attached to that mummy of a Whig party." Furthermore, the paper complained, "he dares not oppose the Fugitive Slave Law—and he would not pledge himself to go against the admission of any more Slave States," both true indictments. Lincoln's obvious overtures to the South during his campaign tour in the fall of 1854 were held against him. Charles H. Ray, a Galena, Illinois, editor who later would be instrumental in Lincoln's presidential nomination, found Lincoln's Southern leanings disturbing. "He is Southern by birth," Ray noted, "Southern in his associations and Southern . . . in his sympathies." His wife, he added, was "of a proslavery family" as were "all his kin." William H. Herndon, Lincoln's law partner who claimed he understood him better than anyone else, found Lincoln's views "too conservative" to satisfy the groundswell of opposition to the Kansas-Nebraska Act. Lincoln, one antislavery leader concluded, "is only a Whig and the people's movement is no Whig triumph."[9]

It was clear even to Lincoln that the cause demanded something more drastic and dramatic than a reorganized Whig party. Soon after Douglas introduced his legislation, a call was issued for a new party that would fuse free soilers, antislavery Whigs, and anti-Nebraska

8. William E. Gienapp, *The Origins of the Republican Party, 1852–1856* (New York, 1987), 82–85; Stanley Harrold, *Gamaliel Bailey and Antislavery Union* (Kent, Ohio, 1986), 163; Wendell Phillips, quoted in Gerteis, *Morality & Unity in American Antislavery Reform*, 131

9. Chicago *Free West*, November 30, December 14, 1854, quoted in Edward Magdol, *Owen Lovejoy: Abolitionist in Congress* (New Brunswick, N.J., 1967), 119; Ray to Elihu B. Washburne, December 24, 1854, quoted in Jay Monaghan, *The Man Who Elected Lincoln* (Indianapolis, 1956), 41–42; Herndon to Jesse W. Weik, October 28, 1885, in Emanuel Hertz, *The Hidden Lincoln: From the Letters and Papers of William H. Herndon* (New York, 1938), 96.

Democrats into a new and unambiguous antislavery organization. To Lincoln, the prospect was alarming. Like Whig leaders in other Northern states, he urged party members to resist the appeals of the fusionists. While some immediate success might be gained, Springfield's Whig editor agreed, "what would be the future of the whigs?" To focus solely on the slavery issue would mean setting aside the platform that had given the party its identity. Lincoln had labored for twenty-five years in behalf of Henry Clay's American System, the program that tied economic development to strong centralized national authority, and he was not prepared to give up that investment. The consequences of fusion—for himself, his party, and the party system—were so serious that he could not but believe that the movement for a new party was an ill-timed, poorly considered aberration.

"There will be, in our opinion, no large third party," assured the *Illinois State Journal*. "There have always been but two large permanent parties in the country; and when the Nebraska matter is disposed of, the members of the Free-Soil party will fall into the ranks of one of the two parties," as indeed they had before.[10]

Nevertheless, Lincoln advised Whigs to "stand with anybody that stands RIGHT," even if it meant standing with the "abolitionist in restoring the Missouri Compromise," suggesting that there were moments when principle must overcome party. His words were put to a test almost immediately. Abolitionist leaders, attending a meeting at the capital to organize the Republican party, decided that Lincoln was ripe for conversion and sought to enlist him in their cause. That was not what Lincoln had had in mind. Herndon recalled years later that he intervened to save Lincoln the embarrassment of having to reject their overtures. He advised Lincoln to leave town and not to return until after the "apostles of Abolitionism had . . . gone to their homes." Lincoln took Herndon's advice and left Springfield, pleading the pressure of legal business in a nearby county. Actually, he embarked on his customary tour of the judicial circuit, but his departure was nonetheless fortuitous. Lincoln recounted the incident during his debates with Douglas four years

10. Springfield *Illinois State Journal*, July 27, 1854.

later and acknowledged the effort to get him into the Republican party. "I would not go in," he declared.[11]

Failing to persuade Lincoln to attend the meeting, the fusionists placed his name on the Republican State Central Committee, even though some of them expressed doubts about the sincerity of his views on slavery. The Douglas press gleefully pounced on the action as proof that Lincoln was an abolitionist after all. Deeply annoyed and perplexed, Lincoln protested that his name had been used without consulting him first. "I suppose my opposition to the principle of slavery is as strong as that of any member of the Republican party," he explained to Ichabod Codding, "but I had also supposed that the *extent* to which I feel authorized to carry that opposition, practically, was not at all satisfactory to that party." His response was equivocal; this time, political expediency overcame principle. Still, he did not ask that his name be removed, and he only implied that he was unwilling to serve. Perhaps the Republicans had misunderstood his position, he suggested. Or had he misunderstood theirs? He was unwilling to commit himself to their cause, but he did not want to alienate them either.[12]

The decisive blow to Lincoln's hopes for restoring vitality to the Whig party was his failure to win election to the United States Senate early in 1855. Even with the quiet encouragement of the Douglas Democrats, who wished to forestall a revolt in their party, Lincoln was unable to garner enough votes. The election of an anti-Nebraska Democrat, besides delivering a serious setback to the Douglas party, was clear evidence that the antislavery movement would not accept Whig leadership. To his keen disappointment, Lincoln learned just how much of a "mummy" his party had become. However he con-

11. Speech at Peoria, Illinois, October 16, 1854, First Debate with Stephen A. Douglas at Ottawa, Illinois, August 21, 1858, in *Collected Works*, II, 273, III, 13; William H. Herndon and Jesse W. Weik, *Herndon's Life of Lincoln*, ed. Paul M. Angle (Cleveland, 1949), 299. For the role of Illinois abolitionists in the early organization of the Republican party, see Victor B. Howard, "The Illinois Republican Party, Part I: A Party Organizer for the Republicans in 1854," *Journal of the Illinois State Historical Society*, LXIV (Summer, 1971), 125–60.

12. Lincoln to Ichabod Codding, November 27, 1854, in *Collected Works*, II, 288. Lincoln's equivocation probably stemmed from his hope that the abolitionist Owen Lovejoy, newly elected member of the state legislature, would support him for the United States Senate. Elihu B. Washburne to Lincoln, January 17, 1855, in Abraham Lincoln Papers, Library of Congress (microfilm); Magdol, *Owen Lovejoy*, 120.

soled himself, he could not escape the feeling that his future in politics was suddenly uncertain. His situation was not unlike that of Seward several months before: "I am too much of an anti-slavery man to be proscribed by anti-slavery men," Seward wrote, "and yet too much of a Whig to be allowed to lead." Lincoln had arrived at a moment of decision as critical as any he had ever faced. His deepest loyalties, sentimental attachments, and political convictions demanded a persevering fidelity to the party of Henry Clay. Yet a realistic appraisal of his political future pushed him in another direction, toward a decision he never expected to make—the abandonment of the Whig middle ground and affiliation with a new, untried, and radical party movement.[13]

The transition would be neither easy nor swift for a man of strong partisan commitments and political ambitions. Lincoln, Herndon impatiently observed, was "proverbially slow in his movements," too slow, one may assume, for his impulsive law partner. But Lincoln was by nature a careful individual, taking no step or making no move without first calculating its impact on his career. As the conflict over slavery moved to a new, more violent stage as Kansans struggled to organize their territory, Lincoln decided to pick up the "lost crumbs" of his neglected law practice and to bide his time. His unsettled state of mind, however, was revealed in his private correspondence. No one, he pleaded, was more anxious than he to halt the expansion of slavery. Yet, he confessed, "the political atmosphere is such . . . that I fear to do any thing, lest I do wrong." With his political future at stake, he could not afford to make a decision he would later regret. There were moments when his uncertainty bordered on paralysis. Just where he stood, he confided to an old friend, was a "disputed point." "I am a whig," he wrote, "but others say there are no whigs, and that I am an abolitionist." But, he protested, he was not an abolitionist either, for "I now do no more than oppose the *extension* of slavery."[14]

13. Seward, May 31, 1854, quoted in Frederick W. Seward, *Seward at Washington*, 231. For details of Lincoln's defeat for senator, see Don E. Fehrenbacher, *Prelude to Greatness: Lincoln in the 1850's* (Stanford, 1962), 37–39; and Robert W. Johannsen, *Stephen A. Douglas* (New York, 1973), 462–64.

14. Herndon and Weik, *Herndon's Life of Lincoln*, 310; Lincoln to Owen Lovejoy, August 11, 1855, Lincoln to Joshua F. Speed, August 24, 1855, in *Collected Works*, II, 316, 322–23.

No more, however, was apparently not enough. How long would it be before the exigencies of sectional politics would force him to move beyond his insistence that the Missouri Compromise be restored and that the spirit of compromise with the South be renewed? The choices seemed to be narrowing. The "mere hatred of slavery" and opposition to the "injustice of the Kansas-Nebraska legislation" were no longer "all that was required of him." There was no longer a place for what he had called the "good old whig ground." Herndon later recalled: "Finding himself drifting about with the disorganized elements . . . it became apparent to Lincoln that if he expected to figure as a leader he must take a stand himself."

Like many Northern Whigs, Lincoln was forced to reassess the direction of his career and to contemplate a move to more radical antislavery and anti-Southern views. The groundwork for such a move had already been laid in his campaign speeches during the fall of 1854. He had established a prospectus for the future, as became an astute politician, with enough flexibility built into it to enable him to modify, shift, or rearrange his priorities. But what good was a prospectus without a party to go with it? Unless he declared himself, he would (in Herndon's language) "forever float about in the great political sea without compass, rudder, or sail." Lincoln did the only thing he could do; he moved by slow and cautious degrees toward an embrace of the more radical posture of the fledgling Republican party. He did so reluctantly, to be sure, and against the advice of some of his Whig friends. As late as November, 1855, the *Illinois State Journal* cited the "utter hopelessness" of cutting loose from the Whig party in favor of one organized "on the single idea of opposition to Slavery." The Republican party in Illinois, commanding but a "very small faction of voters and those only of the most ultra views," the editor predicted, would be "entirely without rank and file" within six months.

Many years later, Lincoln remarked, "I claim not to have controlled events, but confess plainly that events have controlled me." The statement was written during his last year as president, but it could not have been more apt than during the troubled aftermath of the Kansas-Nebraska Act.[15]

15. Herndon and Weik, *Herndon's Life of Lincoln*, 311; Springfield *Illinois State Jour-*

Lincoln was seen once again "mousing about" the libraries in the statehouse, spending all the time his law practice would allow searching for information on the slavery question, or, as his admiring biographers preferred to put it, "vigilantly pursuing the study of the higher phases of the great moral and political struggle." In the meantime, the same developments in Kansas that stimulated the growth of the Republican party were influencing Lincoln's outlook. Newspaper headlines screamed of Bleeding Kansas, of border ruffians and slave conspiracies that made a mockery of the efforts to organize a territorial government. Douglas' doctrine of popular sovereignty, it appeared, was part of a pernicious plot to expand slavery after all. Lincoln even convinced himself that the outrages committed in Kansas had been intended by Douglas from the start. Douglas' zeal to fasten slavery on the territories no longer seemed covert, as Lincoln had once said. A new and bitter anti-South attitude crept into his thinking.

"You know I dislike slavery," Lincoln confided to an old friend. "I hate to see the poor creatures hunted down, and caught, and carried back to their stripes, and unrewarded toils; but I bite my lip and keep quiet." He wondered how much longer the people of the North could continue to "crucify their feelings, in order to maintain their loyalty to the constitution and the Union." Lincoln's once generous view of the dilemma in which Southerners found themselves gave way to cynicism. If Kansas should vote fairly for a slave state, he wrote, he would have to support its admission to the Union. However, if it voted unfairly, as appeared more likely, Kansas would still be admitted, for the South would "bribe enough of our men to carry the day." Southerners, he fancied, could even establish a monarchy if they wished, simply by declaring it to be a *democratic party necessity.*

As Lincoln made the transition from Whig to Republican, his statements became at once more ambivalent and more extreme, perhaps revealing still an uncertain state of mind. His attitude toward the South lost the tone of calm understanding he had so effectively expressed only a year before. While he still reminded audiences that

nal, November 30, 1855; Lincoln to A. G. Hodges, April 4, 1864, in *Collected Works,* VII, 282.

Southerners were no different from them physically and intellectually, he also spoke of a widening gap that had opened between North and South, brought on by the South's "odious institution of slavery." Drawing his perceptions of Southern thinking from George Fitzhugh's anonymous contributions to the Richmond *Enquirer,* Lincoln now charged Southerners with defending slavery on principle and contending that their slaves were better off than free white men in the North. They maintained, moreover, that slavery had a moral right to expand beyond the borders of the slave states. Hints of self-righteousness surfaced as he placed all the onus for the agitation and for fostering ill-will between the sections on Douglas and the South, while absolving Northern antislavery elements from any responsibility for the sectional conflict.[16]

As he studied, pondered, and puzzled over his future course, Lincoln was exposed to conflicting pressures and advice. From Joshua R. Giddings, Ohio's abolitionist member of Congress whom Lincoln knew when he was himself a congressman, came word that the Republican movement was "going forward in every free State" and that only Illinois remained in doubt. Illinoisans were "timid and fearful" because their leaders had not yet embraced the new party. Giddings urged Lincoln to exert his "own personal efforts," assume the lead, and give "direction to those movements which are to determine the next Presidential election." On the other hand, Springfield's Whig editor, resistant to the last, warned that the Republican party, "based upon a single idea," was "so intensely sectional, that its existence could not be continued with safety to the Union." He looked forward to the 1856 election when the "good old Whig party," uniting North and South on a national platform, would once again be in the field.[17]

Lincoln's frustration boiled over in correspondence with George Robertson, former congressman from Kentucky, jurist, and prominent Lexington lawyer, who had argued that restricting slavery to the states where it existed "could neither hasten the peaceful extinc-

---

16. John G., Nicolay and John Hay, *Abraham Lincoln: A History* (10 vols.; New York, 1890), I, 390; Lincoln to Speed, August 24, 1855, Speech at Kalamazoo, Michigan, August 27, 1856, in *Collected Works,* II, 320–22, 362, 364.

17. Joshua R. Giddings to Lincoln, September 15, 1855, in Herndon-Weik Collection, Library of Congress; Springfield *Illinois State Journal,* November 15, 1855.

tion of slavery, nor improve the condition of slaves in the United States." Lincoln, in reply, despaired that slavery could ever be peacefully abolished, for "that spirit which desired the peaceful extinction of slavery" had itself become extinct "with the *occasion* and the *men* of the Revolution." The condition of the slave, he believed, was "as fixed, and hopeless of change for the better, as that of the lost souls of the finally impenitent." Sooner would the "Autocrat of all the Russias" resign his crown and declare all his subjects republicans than would "our American masters" voluntarily free their slaves. In language that would be echoed in a more famous utterance three years later, Lincoln observed that "our political problem now is 'Can we, as a nation, continue together *permanently—forever*—half slave and half free?'" He had no answer to the question. The problem, he lamented, was "too mighty" for him.[18]

The turmoil in Kansas, the increased militancy of the Southern proslavery leadership, the utter hopelessness of Whig fortunes, the rapid rise of Republican strength, and the imminence of the 1856 election, all worked their own peculiar influences on Lincoln's state of mind. His journey into the Republican ranks was almost complete.

Lincoln received his final push from Illinois' abolitionists, who had persisted in their efforts to woo him into their ranks, knowing that his popularity and experience would be invaluable to the new party. Owen Lovejoy wrote him in August, 1855, urging him to join the Republican party, and was heartened when Lincoln replied in a tone that was much more conciliatory than the one he had used with Codding the previous November (before the senatorial election). "Not even *you* are more anxious to prevent the extension of slavery than I," he wrote Lovejoy. He would "'fuse' with any body," provided it was on ground he felt was right. "I believe the opponents of slavery extension could now do this." He himself was deterred from doing so, he said, solely because many of his "old political and per-

18. Speech of Mr. Robertson, of Kentucky, on the Bill to Establish the Territorial Government of Arkansas, February 18, 1819, in George Robertson, *Scrap Book on Law and Politics, Men and Times* (Lexington, 1855), 26; Lincoln to George Robertson, August 15, 1855, in *Complete Works*, II, 317–18. For more on Lincoln's correspondence with Robertson, see William H. Townsend, *Lincoln and the Bluegrass* (Lexington, 1955), 216–19.

sonal friends" had joined ranks with the Know-Nothings, and he did not want to risk antagonizing them, an excuse that even Lincoln recognized as weak.[19]

To satisfy those who doubted the sincerity of Lincoln's antislavery views, Zebina Eastman, editor of the abolitionist paper *Free West*, visited Springfield and talked with some of Lincoln's friends. Lincoln, he was assured, "was all right on the Negro question." Since there was a possibility that Lincoln would become a "competitor of Judge Douglas" if he joined the Republicans, Eastman sought confirmation from Herndon. Lincoln's law partner dispelled all doubts. Lincoln was an attentive reader of Eastman's newspaper, he was a "great reader" of other abolition papers, and he believed in the Declaration of Independence. "Although he does not say much," Herndon noted, "you may depend upon it, Mr. Lincoln is all right." When it became necessary, he would "speak so that he will be understood."[20]

Years later, Herndon claimed credit for Lincoln's move into the Republican party in the spring of 1856, when he signed Lincoln's name to the call for a county convention without permission. "I forged his name," he wrote. "I was determined to make him take a stand, if he would not do it willingly." Lincoln, who was out of Springfield at the time, decided to let it stand: "All right; go ahead. Will meet you—radicals and all." From that moment, Herndon recalled, the "conservative spirits who hovered around Springfield no longer held control of the political fortunes of Abraham Lincoln." Herndon's memory, however, betrayed him, for Lincoln had already made his move when he attended a meeting of anti-Nebraska editors in Decatur on February 22, to decide on strategy for the state and national campaigns later in the year. He was the only non-editor in

19. Magdol, *Owen Lovejoy*, 130–31; Lincoln to Lovejoy, August 11, 1855, in *Collected Works*, II, 316. Unlike many Northern Whigs, Lincoln was unequivocal in his rejection of Know-Nothingism as an alternative to the Whig party. "Of their principles," he wrote Lovejoy, "I think little better than I do of those of the slavery extensionists." See also Lincoln to Joshua F. Speed, August 24, 1855, in *Collected Works*, II, 323.

20. Zebina Eastman, "History of the Anti-Slavery Agitation, and the Growth of the Liberty and Republican Parties in the State of Illinois," quoted in Magdol, *Owen Lovejoy*, 132–33; Herndon to Weik, September 24, 1890, in Hertz, *The Hidden Lincoln*, 253–54.

attendance. Lincoln scholars have generally regarded the editors' convention as the "real beginning" of the Republican party in Illinois, thereby enabling them to view Lincoln as one of the party's founders. The Douglas press at the time, however, had it right: Lincoln had responded to the "tap of the fusion drum" and had demonstrated his readiness to join the Republican ranks. Lincoln had already crossed his Rubicon over two months before Herndon put his name on the convention call.[21]

Lincoln had chosen his moment well, and like everything else he did, his move was the result of long and careful calculation. On the day the editors met in Decatur, Republican delegates from the free states of the North gathered in Pittsburgh to establish an organization capable of competing in the coming presidential contest. To Lincoln, it was a signal that the fusion movement had attained sufficient strength and respectability to take its place as a major element in the party system. The Republican party no longer appeared to be a temporary phenomenon. Fortunately for Lincoln, the radical leadership of the Illinois party had gone to Pittsburgh and was not in attendance at Decatur, for Lincoln had not only decided to join the party but had also determined to control its direction. What he had failed to achieve with a reborn Whig party, an organization and platform that could unite North and South, he might accomplish as a Republican.

Barely three months before, the *Illinois State Journal*, still seeking to persuade its readers that there was no "sound reason" for the Republican party, proposed that all the opponents of the "Pierce and Douglas dynasty" unite on a national platform "wide and broad enough to receive, not only the friends of good government at the North, but the true and conservative men of the South" in order to bring Democratic party hegemony to an end. The platform adopted at the editors' meeting, which Lincoln helped to draft, came close to fulfilling the *Journal's* prescription. Looking very much like a North-South compromise, it stipulated that slavery was to be protected in

21. Call for Republican Convention, May 10, 1856, in *Collected Works*, II, 340; Herndon, quoted in David Donald, *Lincoln's Herndon* (New York, 1948), 86; Herndon and Weik, *Herndon's Life of Lincoln*, 311–12; Fehrenbacher, *Prelude to Greatness*, 44–45; Paul M. Angle, *Lincoln, 1854–1861* (Springfield, 1933), 112; Springfield *Illinois State Register*, February 25, 1856.

the slaveholding states, the three-fifths clause in the Constitution was to be respected, and the Fugitive Slave Act was to be enforced, in return for which the South would agree to the restoration of the Missouri Compromise and the restriction of slavery to the limits established in 1850. "We hold that our General Government is imbued throughout its whole organization with the spirit of liberty, as set forth originally in the Declaration of Independence," the platform concluded, and "that it recognizes FREEDOM as the *rule*, and SLAVERY as the exception"—the "freedom national doctrine" of Chase and Lincoln. The Republican party, at least in its Illinois incarnation, might yet occupy that "good old whig ground." [22]

Although the results of the Decatur meeting were not exactly what the abolitionists had in mind when they tried to persuade Lincoln to join their movement, they needed the organization and strength which Lincoln and his Whig friends could bring to the party and acquiesced in its new and more conservative tone. There were, to be sure, misgivings among some who were especially disturbed by Lincoln's refusal to demand the repeal of the Fugitive Slave Act, to support the abolition of slavery in the District of Columbia, and to oppose the admission of new slave states. Nonetheless, political realities overcame their doubts. Eastman, speaking for the radical leadership, observed that "there was no longer any opposition to Mr. Lincoln from the most radical of the abolitionists," for they now "understood him" and "knew that he was wholly with them."

Lincoln would not have agreed that he was "wholly with them," but he too was adjusting to political realities. Some of his Whig friends balked at an association with abolitionists and were bothered

22. Springfield *Illinois State Journal*, November 28, 1855, February 27, 1856; Reinhard H. Luthin, "Abraham Lincoln Becomes a Republican," *Political Science Quarterly*, LIX (September, 1944), 430. See also Paul Selby, "The Editorial Convention, February 22, 1856," *Transactions of the McLean County Historical Society*, III (Bloomington, 1900), 30–43; and Victor B. Howard, "The Illinois Republican Party, Part II: The Party Becomes Conservative, 1855–1856," *Journal of the Illinois State Historical Society*, LXIV (Autumn, 1971), 293–301. The purpose of the Decatur meeting was to issue a call for a statewide convention, to meet at the end of May, and to make plans for the nomination of a state ticket. The label "Republican" was scrupulously avoided in favor of "anti-Nebraska" in order to eliminate any radical association and to appeal to as wide a spectrum of opposition to the Kansas-Nebraska Act as possible. Gienapp, *Origins of the Republican Party*, 289.

by the sectional nature of the Republican party. To allay their suspicions (as well as his own), Lincoln felt that the party must be molded in the Whig image. "Our party," he remarked, "is fresh from Kentucky and must not be forced to radical measures," by which he meant that the spirit of Henry Clay must be its moving force. "Nine tenths of the Anti-Nebraska votes have to come from old whigs," he reminded Lyman Trumbull. "In setting stakes, is it safe to disregard them?" The abolitionists and the anti-Nebraska Democrats, he was convinced, "will go with us anyway." Within two years, he was telling Illinoisans that "there was no difference" between the principles of the Whig party "as expounded by its great leader, Henry Clay," and those of the Republican party. To those who continued to complain that they were in the company of men "who have long been known as abolitionists," Lincoln replied with one of his basic political rules of thumb: "What care we how many may feel disposed to labor for our cause?" He would accept support from wherever he could get it, so long as he himself was not tarred with the abolitionist brush.[23]

Once Lincoln had decided to join the Republican movement, he threw himself into the cause with all the vigor and dedication he could muster. The months of uncertainty that followed his defeat for the Senate early in 1855 gave way before a new surge of political energy. "If ever a man committed himself by deed and word, voluntarily and openly," Fehrenbacher has noted, Lincoln did so in 1856. There was much at stake, both personally and politically. When members of the editors' convention proposed that he accept nomination for state governor, he quickly demurred; but when he was toasted as "our next candidate for the U.S. Senate," the chords of ambition began vibrating once again. "That sentiment I am in favor of," Lincoln replied. Douglas' second term as senator would expire in two years, and the prospect of a race against the Little

23. Zebina Eastman, quoted in Magdol, *Owen Lovejoy*, 147; Lincoln, quoted in Albert J. Beveridge, *Abraham Lincoln, 1809–1858* (2 vols.; Boston, 1928), II, 368; Lincoln to Lyman Trumbull, June 7, 1856, Speech at Tremont, Illinois, August 30, 1858, Speech at Kalamazoo, Michigan, August 27, 1856, in *Collected Works*, II, 343, III, 77, II, 366. Lincoln continued to receive advice from his friends to maintain his distance from the abolitionists; see, for example, Henry C. Whitney's warnings, July 31, 1858, in Abraham Lincoln Papers, Library of Congress.

Giant held untold opportunities for political advancement no matter how the contest would be decided.[24]

As a Republican, Lincoln soon learned that maintaining an old Whig, conservative posture was easier to preach than to practice. The demands which Republican party unity placed upon him, the continuing violence in Kansas, the caning of Charles Sumner by a South Carolina congressman, and the threats of secession that were hurled by Southern fire-eaters, all militated against a platform that would promote sectional harmony between North and South. When the Republican party met in its first national convention in Philadelphia in June, 1856, to nominate a slate of candidates for the presidency and vice-presidency, it adopted a platform that has been described as an "unusually radical document." Condemning slavery as a relic of barbarism, the delegates endorsed the Declaration of Independence, declared that the Founding Fathers had committed the nation to a policy of freedom over slavery, and demanded that Congress prohibit slavery in all the territories (thereby moving beyond the restoration of the Missouri Compromise and brushing aside the Compromise of 1850). Southerners reacted with astonishment and outrage. The new party, they said, had proclaimed its "avowed and unrelenting hostility to the domestic institutions and the equal constitutional rights of the Southern States." With a platform deliberately anti-Southern as well as antislavery, Republicans appeared to stand "on the one simple, exclusive, distinct idea of hostility to the South." The abolitionists were delighted, for they saw in the platform a statement that could justify a "wide variety of measures that would weaken slavery."

Like the abolitionists, Lincoln found it necessary to adjust to the political realities that followed his affiliation with the Republican party. Although he made no comment on the tone of his party's first platform (at least none has been found), he clearly began to move toward the harsh anti-Southern stance adopted by the Republicans.

24. Fehrenbacher, *Prelude to Greatness*, 44; Speech at Decatur, Illinois, February 22, 1856, in *Collected Works*, II, 333. It seems clear that Lincoln was running for Douglas' Senate seat at least two years before the expiration of Douglas' term; see Robert W. Johannsen, "The Lincoln-Douglas Campaign of 1858: Background and Perspective," in Johannsen, *The Frontier, the Union, and Stephen A. Douglas* (Urbana, 1989), 228–48.

In spite of the loud denials, the Republican party was in fact a sectional party, sectional in its membership, its platform, and its appeal, the very kind of geographical party that Lincoln once feared would sound the knell of the Union. Opponents, principally Stephen A. Douglas, were quick to emphasize the contrast between the new party and the national Whig organization it apparently replaced. The sectionalism charge, Lincoln conceded, was the "most difficult objection" Republicans had to face. That it bothered him seems clear from the frequency and warmth with which he tried to counter it. He would later insist that the Republican party had penetrated the slaveholding South, but a few kindred souls in the border states did not a party make. He finally resolved the issue by placing responsibility for the sectional character of the Republican party on the Southerners themselves, for, as he said, the party would cease to be sectional if only they would cease their hostility toward it and embrace its position.[25]

The breach between Lincoln and the South widened as his rhetoric assumed a more strident tone. He buckled on his armor, as he had put it, for John C. Frémont, and made over fifty speeches, in and out of Illinois, during the 1856 campaign. The only issue before the people, he proclaimed, was the issue of "freedom or slavery," and he urged the voters to join him and his party in halting slavery's aggressions against the republic. There was no room in his arguments for shadings or subtleties. Those who would not join him in his crusade against slavery were obviously proslavery. The question of whether slavery should be allowed to spread into the new territories or whether it should be restricted, gave way to a more fundamental query, "Shall the Government of the United States prohibit slavery in the United States?"

25. William J. Cooper, Jr., *Liberty and Slavery: Southern Politics to 1860* (New York, 1983), 256; Gienapp, *Origins of the Republican Party*, 335–37; Speech at Clinton, Illinois, July 27, 1858, Speech at Leavenworth, Kansas, December 3, 1859, in *Collected Works*, II, 526, III, 501. For one of Lincoln's more vigorous efforts to refute the sectionalism charge, see his Fragment on Sectionalism, ca. July 23, 1856, in *Collected Works*, II, 349–53. In some ways, the sectional nature of the Republican party worked to Lincoln's advantage, for it freed him of the need to shape his arguments to a national constituency. While he remained mindful of differences in emphasis on the slavery issue within the Republican party, his appeal, with only a few ineffective exceptions, was always to the North.

The choice facing the electorate was clear, for there was no mistaking the enemy. The power of slavery threatened to place the government "on a new track." Slavery, he warned, "is to be made a ruling element in our government." Either "we must submit, and allow slavery to triumph," or "we must triumph over the black demon." The choice was one Lincoln would formalize and make famous two years later, in a statement that professed an irrepressible conflict. With the exaggerated reports of "Bleeding Kansas" confronting Northern readers, his warnings fell on receptive audiences. The crisis, it seemed, was at hand, the danger was acute, and the simple restoration of the Missouri Compromise was no longer by itself the prescription for cleansing the republic.

Yet, with Lincoln, things were not always what they seemed to be. If his audiences felt that he was proposing an attack against slavery in the states where it existed, that illusion was quickly dispelled following the election. As the excitement of the campaign subsided, he calmly assured the party faithful that it was not true—indeed, it was an "unmixed and unmitigated falsehood"—that Republicans wished to alter the "domestic institutions of existing States." [26]

Was it possible for Republicans to have it both ways? To "triumph over the black demon" while leaving it untouched in the states? Some Republicans made no effort to conceal their desire to achieve the immediate abolition of slavery in the states, while others recoiled in horror at the very suggestion of abolition. Both sides were important to Republican success; each, Lincoln knew, had to be recognized. But how? The answer lay in a synthesis that would bridge the differences, enabling him to argue both the abolition of slavery in the United States *and* the constitutional and legal protection of slavery in the states where it existed. If the argument at times appeared to be ambiguous—well, that was in the nature of politics.

Lincoln first brought the concept of the "ultimate extinction" of slavery into his argument following the 1856 election, at a time when the Dred Scott decision and the controversy over the admission of Kansas as a slave state under the Lecompton constitution

26. Speech at Decatur, Illinois, February 22, 1856, Autobiography Written for John L. Scripps, June, 1860, Speech at Chicago, Illinois, July 19, 1856, Speech at Kalamazoo, Michigan, August 27, 1856, Speech at a Republican Banquet, Chicago, December 10, 1856, in *Collected Works*, II, 333, IV, 67, II, 349, 361, 365–66, 384–85.

were driving political discussion into an ever more dangerous polarization. The Supreme Court, he believed, had changed the ground rules and widened the conflict by declaring that *all* the territories must be open to the expansion of slavery. In one sense, ultimate extinction was a response to the court's decision. It was also a step toward a more radical stance, linking his demand for the restriction of slavery to the total elimination of slavery everywhere. He proposed as a matter of deliberate policy to speed slavery's demise in the Southern states by depriving the institution of its nurture. Lincoln recalled, rather belatedly, that he had believed that slavery was in the course of ultimate extinction all along, which explained why he had said so little about it before 1854. Once again, it was in the origins of the republic that he found the provenance for his belief. "All I have asked or desired anywhere," he explained, "is that it [slavery] should be placed back again upon the basis that the fathers of our government originally placed it upon." By readopting "the policy of the fathers," he declared, "I have no doubt that it *would* become extinct, for all time to come." [27]

Lincoln's argument rested on several assumptions that had long been held by antislavery advocates: that slavery required the ability to expand in order to survive; that if slavery were restricted, no additional slave states would ever be admitted; that if slavery were restricted, the slaveholding South would be isolated and reduced to the status of a permanent minority in the nation; and that the pressures against slavery and for its elimination in the states would become irresistible. But by what means would slavery then become extinct? Lincoln was never clear. It would, he suggested, "dwindle out" and die; or the Southerners themselves would end the institution by direct state action. Critics were not convinced, and rejected his explanations as too vague. If, as Lincoln maintained, slavery would be extremely difficult to get rid of if it were allowed into the territories, then how much more difficult would it be to eliminate

27. Fragment of a Speech, May 18, 1858, Speech at Chicago, Illinois, July 10, 1858, Third Debate with Stephen A. Douglas at Jonesboro, Illinois, September 15, 1858, in *Collected Works*, II, 453, 492, III, 117. The "Fragment" in which the phrase was apparently first used was misdated by the editors of the *Collected Works*. Internal evidence suggests that it was written earlier than May 18, possibly in December, 1857, in response to Douglas' December 9 speech in the Senate against the Lecompton constitution.

slavery in the states, where its foothold was so much more secure? Douglas found Lincoln's argument both obscure and ambiguous, and asked how Lincoln was going to put slavery "in the course of ultimate extinction everywhere, if he does not intend to interfere with it in the States where it exists." On the latter point, however, Lincoln was unyielding. He did not mean, he protested, that the national government held the power of emancipation, and he reacted angrily against those who would so misconstrue his words. Writing to John L. Scripps, a Chicago Republican editor who observed that even some Republicans were uneasy, Lincoln emphasized that he had used the phrase carefully and deliberately, never once dreaming that it could be interpreted as asserting the power to interfere with slavery where it existed. "I have declared a thousand times," he wrote, "and now repeat that, in my opinion, neither the General Government, nor any other power outside of the slave states, can constitutionally or rightfully interfere with slaves or slavery where it already exists."[28]

What did Lincoln mean by "ultimate"? Again, he was ambivalent. The ultimate extinction of slavery, he advised, would not be accomplished in a day, a year, or in several years. It "may not be completely attained within the term of my natural life." He did not expect it to occur in less than a hundred years, and on one occasion he seemed to feel slavery might never be rendered extinct. "But whether it should ever become extinct or not," he declared, it was important to live up to "all the guarantees of the Constitution" that protected the slaveholders. Lincoln used the term *ultimate* to signify inevitability. Although he could not put a time period on it, he was certain that the extinction of slavery was inevitable, that it would be accomplished "in God's own good time." He was equally certain that slavery would be "going out of existence in the way best for both the black and the white races," gradually over a very long period of time. In the meantime, the sectional conflict would cease, and the republic would return to the condition intended by the Fathers. He

28. Fragment: Notes for Speeches, ca. August 21, 1858, Speech at Beloit, Wisconsin, October 1, 1859, Speech at Janesville, Wisconsin, October 1, 1859, Seventh and Last Debate with Stephen A. Douglas at Alton, Illinois, October 15, 1858 (Douglas' Reply), Lincoln to John L. Scripps, June 23, 1858, in *Collected Works*, II, 551, III, 483, 485, 323, II, 471.

asked what "milder way" there could be to rid the nation of what he was increasingly calling this "vast moral evil." In his letter to George Robertson, Lincoln wondered if the nation could continue "*permanently—forever*—half slave and half free." He now offered at least a partial answer: perhaps not permanently or forever, but at least for a very long time.[29]

Although Lincoln had little influence on the party organization outside his own state, he came to view his doctrine of ultimate extinction as a test of Republican loyalty. Inasmuch as the extinction of slavery was far in the future, he urged patience as the most important Republican virtue. Directing his words toward the party's radicals, he warned that any Republican who was impatient with the necessity of leaving slavery in the Southern states alone or who did not recognize the legal and constitutional guarantees that had been "thrown around" the institution, would be invited to leave the party—or as Lincoln more tactfully put it, was "misplaced standing with us." The doctrine did its job, for by 1860 even the outspoken antislavery New York *Tribune* predicted the ultimate extinction of slavery "by the operation of natural causes, and in the peaceful legislation of the people of the States where it exists. Such is the orderly and conservative policy of Abraham Lincoln and of the Republican party."[30]

That Lincoln should have felt the need for a party test was in part a consequence of an unexpected turn of events just at the time he

29. Fourth Debate with Stephen A. Douglas at Charleston, Illinois, September 18, 1858, Fragment on the Struggle Against Slavery, ca. July 1858, Speech at Greenville, Illinois, September 13, 1858, First Debate with Stephen A. Douglas at Ottawa, Illinois, August 21, 1858, Speech at Bloomington, Illinois, September 4, 1858, Speech at Chicago, Illinois, July 10, 1858, in *Collected Works*, III, 181, II, 482, III, 96, 18, 89, II, 494. A little more than a year after Lincoln's death, a close friend provided some perspective on the policy of ultimate extinction. Lincoln's "whole life," he wrote, "was a calculation of the law of forces and ultimate results." Certain results "to which certain causes tended," Lincoln believed, were inevitable and could neither be hastened nor impeded. Convinced that the agitation over slavery would result inevitably in its utter overthrow, Lincoln placed himself on the side of inevitability. "His tactics were to get himself in the right place and remain there still until events would find him in that place." Leonard Swett to Herndon, July 17, 1866, in Hertz, *The Hidden Lincoln*, 296.

30. Sixth Debate with Stephen A. Douglas at Quincy, Illinois, October 13, 1858, in *Collected Works*, III, 255; New York *Tribune*, quoted in Charleston *Mercury*, June 2, 1860.

was preparing to make his run for Douglas' senate seat. In late 1857, Douglas assumed a bold (and some said, courageous) stand against the effort to admit Kansas to the Union as a slave state, denouncing the move as a travesty on popular sovereignty and alienating President James Buchanan and the Southern Democrats. Republicans were delighted. Many of them now saw Douglas' popular sovereignty in a different light, not as a license to spread slavery (as Lincoln maintained) but as an effective means for restricting slavery. Suddenly, the Little Giant was being hailed as a champion of freedom in the territories. Lincoln, who had been carefully building support for the senate race, was, to say the least, alarmed. Influential Eastern Republicans urged the party in Illinois to back Douglas and allow him to be re-elected without opposition. The praise that was heaped upon Douglas, Lincoln feared, would result in defections from the Republican ranks. There were disturbing reports that Douglas would assume "steep free-soil ground, and furiously assail the administration" when he returned to stump the state. In classic understatement, Lincoln moaned, "political matters just now bear a very *mixed* and *incongruous* aspect." His future career seemed in jeopardy.[31]

The curious political configuration during the 1858 senatorial campaign in Illinois—that is, Republicans outside the state urging that Douglas not be opposed, Southern Democrats and President Buchanan providing indirect encouragement to Lincoln—placed an unwonted burden on the state's Republican leadership. For Lincoln, the crisis was severe, for he believed the integrity, even the existence, of the party, not just in Illinois but throughout the North, depended upon the outcome of the election.[32] It was urgent that Republicans be discouraged from defecting to Douglas' side, especially the conservative old Whigs to whom Douglas' stand would be

31. Lincoln to Lyman Trumbull, December 28, 1857, Lincoln to Elihu B. Washburne, May 27, 1858, in *Collected Works*, II, 430, 455.
32. Writing to Salmon P. Chase following his defeat for the Senate early in 1859, Lincoln declared that in making the race, even though defeated, he had saved the Republican cause from annihilation in Illinois and from being "demoralized, and prostrated everywhere for years." Because he challenged Douglas, the "Republican star gradually rises higher everywhere." Lincoln to Chase, April 30, 1859, in *Collected Works*, III, 378.

most appealing. The differences between Douglas and the Republican party were to be so sharply drawn and emphasized that Lincoln's supporters would find it morally impossible to switch sides. At the same time, it was necessary to weaken Douglas nationally by exposing his differences with the Southern Democrats, thus denying him the support of the South in the next presidential election. It was a strategy that only a consummate politician like Lincoln could pull off.

Declaring that Douglas' popular sovereignty rested on an attitude of indifference toward slavery and on the conviction that slavery was as good as freedom and therefore ought to be expanded, Lincoln invoked a moral argument against the institution, a higher law to which Republicans must remain faithful. He was merciless in pointing out to party members that an unbridgeable moral gulf separated them from Douglas. The contest was not only between freedom and slavery; it was even more importantly a struggle between right and wrong. There was no middle ground. Those "who think slavery a wrong" were arrayed against "those who do not think it wrong." Lincoln shrewdly stopped short of charging Douglas with believing that slavery was right, but he left little doubt that the Little Giant's actions tended to confirm that view. Republicans, he said, considered slavery to be a moral, social, and political wrong, and believed the institution was an "unqualified evil to the negro, to the white man, to the soil, and to the State." There was only one way for Republicans to think and act. The Republican party, Lincoln insisted without equivocation, was the party of morality, whose platform against slavery was sanctioned by God, while Douglas stood with the forces of evil.

Lincoln, moreover, enlisted the spirit of Henry Clay in his cause, in part to give his argument an orthodox Whig flavor. Noting that Clay, although a slaveholder, believed slavery to be the "greatest of human evils," he recalled Clay's 1827 speech on behalf of colonization; indeed, he quoted from the speech so frequently and so freely that people assumed the words were originally his. Clay had charged that those who would resist "ultimate emancipation" must (in Lincoln's version) "go back to the era of our independence and muzzle the cannon which thunders its annual joyous return; they must blow out the moral lights around us; they must penetrate the human soul, and eradicate there the love of liberty."[33]

Lincoln reinforced his moral argument further with an appeal to the natural rights doctrine of the Declaration of Independence, a tactic that threatened to derail his effort for it opened him once again to the charge that he favored racial equality. There is no reason to question the sincerity of Lincoln's belief that slavery was a "gross outrage on the law of nature," inasmuch as it violated the spirit and letter of the Declaration. He had often insisted that the Negro was as much entitled to the enumerated natural rights as the white person, and that in the enjoyment of these rights, he was the "*equal of every living man.*"

Yet when pressed by Douglas, Lincoln quickly qualified his statements. He responded with anger and impatience to the charge that he favored racial equality. "I have no purpose," he declared, "to introduce political and social equality between the white and black races." Once he reacted to the charge, however, his explanations only drew him more deeply into ambiguity. He conceded that the Declaration of Independence did not mean that all men were created equal in all respects. Indeed, he contended, "there is a physical difference between the two [races], which in my judgment will probably forever forbid their living together upon the footing of perfect equality." He expressed his distaste for all the quibbling (Lincoln's word) about "this race and that race and the other race being inferior," though he did not hesitate to assert that he, "as much as any other man," was in favor of having the "superior position assigned to the white race." The words of the Declaration, he suggested, were to be understood as a "standard maxim for free society," an abstract truth rather than a "legal obligation." In any case, the promise of the

---

33. Speech at Edwardsville, Illinois, September 11, 1858, Sixth Debate with Stephen A. Douglas at Quincy, Illinois, October 13, 1858, First Debate with Stephen A. Douglas at Ottawa, Illinois, August 21, 1858, Speech at Bloomington, Illinois, September 4, 1858, in *Collected Works,* III, 92, 254, 29, 89. Douglas also employed references to Henry Clay in his appeal to old Whigs, a tactic to which Lincoln objected with indignation. Speech at Bath, Illinois, August 16, 1858, in *Collected Works,* II, 543. Clay's speech, delivered on January 20, 1827, is in Mary W. M. Hargreaves and James F. Hopkins, eds., *The Papers of Henry Clay* (Lexington, 1959–), VI, 94.

Declaration of Independence was in its argument *against* slavery, rather than *for* racial equality.[34]

The story of Lincoln's campaign against Douglas in 1858 is a familiar one. Lincoln's strategy was successful. While he held Republicans to the support of the party's ticket, he also weakened Douglas' strength outside Illinois by exposing his differences with the Buchanan administration and Southern Democrats. Douglas was reelected to the United States Senate by the state legislature, but the popular vote in the state went to Lincoln and his party. Lincoln's statements in the campaign were publicized in the Republican press, quelling any doubts Republicans might have had about his candidacy for Douglas' senate seat, and were reprinted in 1860 to aid the party's presidential campaign. Few politicians had so dramatically articulated the moral stakes in the sectional conflict or had so effectively employed moral arguments for the achievement of political ends. Lincoln was correct in his assumption that his career would receive an enormous boost from his race against Douglas, whether he won election or not. It was not long before he was proposed as a candidate for the presidency itself. Writing about Lincoln's decision to join the Republican party, Don Fehrenbacher has stated that "there is nothing to indicate that he had any serious misgivings about it afterward."[35] Indeed, he did not. His journey from the middle ground of a national party to the more radical ground of a sectional anti-Southern organization, although undertaken with some trepidation, was smooth and politically rewarding.

Two weeks after Lincoln's nomination for president in the spring of 1860, the New York *Herald* (not a friendly paper) asked what it called the "Question of the Day"—"Is the Republican Candidate for the Presidency an Abolitionist?" The question had been asked in both North and South ever since Lincoln's position became known.

34. Speech at Springfield, Illinois, October 4, 1854, Speech at Springfield, Illinois, June 26, 1857, First Debate with Stephen A. Douglas at Ottawa, Illinois, August 21, 1858, Speech at Chicago, Illinois, July 10, 1858, Fourth Debate with Stephen A. Douglas at Charleston, Illinois, September 18, 1858, Lincoln to James N. Brown, October 18, 1858, in *Collected Works*, II, 245, 405–406, III, 16, II, 501, III, 146, 327–28.
35. Fehrenbacher, *Prelude to Greatness*, 35.

To Southerners, the answer was obvious. A New Orleans editor, after examining some of Lincoln's speeches for the first time, concluded that he was a "thorough radical Abolitionist, without exception or qualification." A Georgia paper viewed Lincoln as a "degenerate son of the South turned abolitionist," ten times more dangerous because of his Southern roots than if he had been born in the North. To a Charleston, South Carolina, paper, Lincoln was "as much an abolitionist as are Garrison, Gerrit Smith, or Wendell Phillips."[36]

The charge was not a new one, for it had been made many times before by his opponents, notably Stephen A. Douglas. Lincoln vigorously denied that he was an abolitionist, and Americans ever since have taken his word for it. The very word "abolitionist" was an "odious epithet" to him. "I know of no word in the language," he commented in 1856, "that has been used so much as that one 'abolitionist,' having no definition." The word had no meaning, he stated, unless it be taken "as designating a person who is abolishing something." That designation, he felt, could not be applied to him. Nor, he insisted, could it be applied to his party. In 1856, he denied that any supporters of Frémont were abolitionists and maintained that there was not a single man in Kansas "who was an abolitionist—for what was there to be abolished?" Later, in his inaugural address as president, he made the extraordinary claim that no individual in the Republican party, to his knowledge, had ever "avowed, or entertained, a purpose to destroy or to interfere with the property of the Southern people."[37]

Insofar as the word "abolitionist" meant an immediatist, that is, one who demanded the immediate abolition of slavery wherever it existed, Lincoln was right—he was not an abolitionist. But ought the word to be defined only in that rather narrow sense? As Southerners became familiar with Lincoln's arguments (in many instances, not until his speeches were circulated during the 1860 campaign),

36. New York *Herald*, June 2, 1860; New Orleans *Daily Crescent*, November 12, 1860, in Dwight L. Dumond, ed., *Southern Editorials on Secession* (New York, 1931), 230–31; Milledgeville (Ga.) *Federal Union*, May 29, 1860; Charleston *Mercury*, September 7, 1860.

37. Springfield *Illinois State Journal*, October 19, 1854; Speech at Kalamazoo, Michigan, August 27, 1856, First Inaugural Address, March 4, 1861, in *Collected Works*, II, 365, IV, 258.

they noted with some concern the ambiguities in his public statements: his charge that slavery was evil and wrong and should be
dealt with as a wrong, yet his oft-repeated willingness to protect it
in those areas where it existed; his demand on some occasions that
slavery be restricted only in new territories, and on other occasions
that it be eliminated in all territories, present as well as future; his
deep devotion to the principle that all men are created equal, yet his
inflexible opposition to the political and social equality of the black
and white races; and finally, and most important of all, his strong
denials that he was an abolitionist, yet his repeated insistence that
slavery be placed in the course of ultimate extinction. Southerners,
who had long regarded Northern antislavery politicians as "hypocritical scoundrels," looked upon Lincoln with suspicion, if not outright fear and hostility.

Ultimate extinction held within its meaning Lincoln's concern for
order and stability (he had always felt that the abolition movement
threatened disorder and instability), as well as his recognition that
legal and constitutional guarantees protected slavery from any quick
and easy elimination. But ultimate extinction was also a convenient
political instrument for binding the more extreme antislavery elements in the North to his party. It was little more than a euphemism
for abolition, a sugar-coated abolition perhaps, but abolition all the
same. It was as close to an outright abolition stance as Lincoln dared
to go without arousing the opposition of the party's conservative
members. It enabled him to advance what was in effect an abolition
argument, without at the same time identifying himself with abolitionists. According to Noah Webster's *American Dictionary of the En-
glish Language*, 1848 edition (if that can be taken as a guide), the
words *extinction* and *abolition* had identical meanings: destruction, a
putting an end to.

To the South, ultimate extinction sounded a clear and ominous
warning. Lincoln, it was said, promised abolitionism when he proposed to place the government on the side of freedom and thus to
insure the ultimate extinction of slavery. He had revealed the intention of his party "to destroy slavery, if not boldly, at least by indirect
and slow approaches." Ultimate extinction meant ultimate emancipation. It was Lincoln's plan for the abolition of slavery everywhere.
Abolitionism was the "informing and actuating soul" of the Repub-

lican party. Having proclaimed slavery to be a moral evil, Lincoln would be untrue to his own principles if he did not bend all of his power and energy to its elimination. Following Lincoln's election as president, one Southern writer predicted, "When Lincoln is in place, Garrison will be in power." The ultimate extinction of slavery, Southerners were confident, would mean the ultimate extinction of the South.

How did the New York *Herald* answer its question of the day? Lincoln's speeches, the paper declared, proved beyond doubt that he was an abolitionist. In view of Lincoln's repeated denials, however, the editor proposed that the word "extinctionist" would suit him better. Abolitionist or extinctionist? To most Americans, it was a distinction without a difference.[38]

38. Kenneth S. Greenberg, *Masters and Statesmen: The Political Culture of American Slavery* (Baltimore, 1985), 130 (for the phrase "hypocritical scoundrels"); *Southern Literary Messenger,* XXXII (January, 1861), 71; *Southern Literary Messenger,* XXXII (February, 1861), 81; New Orleans *Daily Crescent,* December 14, 1860, in Dumond, ed., *Southern Editorials on Secession,* 332; Charleston *Courier,* November 13, 1860; Rev. Benjamin Morgan Palmer, "Slavery a Divine Trust. Duty of the South to Preserve and Perpetuate It," in Palmer, *Fast Day Sermons; or, The Pulpit on the State of the Country* (New York, 1861), 75–77; New York *Herald,* June 2, 1860.

3

The Irrepressible Conflict

On October 25, 1858, William H. Seward, campaigning for Republican candidates in the important off-year election, delivered a speech in Rochester that brought a new phrase and concept into the rhetoric of sectional politics. The country, he said, possessed two radically different, antagonistic, and incompatible political systems, the one based on slavery and the other on freedom, the one intolerable, unjust, and inhuman, the other conforming to divine law. Between these "opposing and enduring forces," there existed "an irrepressible conflict," a conflict that was incapable of accommodation. All efforts to compromise the differences would prove "vain and ephemeral." The United States, he declared, "must and will, sooner or later, become either entirely a slave-holding nation, or entirely a free-labor nation." Moving to the heart of his message, Seward maintained that only the Republican party could save the country. Under Republican leadership, a revolution had been initiated, and "revolutions never go backward." On the contrary, the revolution would go forward "steadily and perseveringly," until those who had betrayed freedom and the moral law would "by one decisive blow" be overthrown forever.

The language was unequivocal and menacing, portending the inevitable and violent overthrow of slavery. The words, uttered by the front-runner for the 1860 Republican nomination for the presidency, were closely scrutinized in both the North and the South. Their meaning was unmistakable. Abolitionists were delighted, Republicans were distressed, and Southerners were in an uproar. The New York *Herald* described the speech as a "bloody manifesto" and Seward as an "arch agitator." His election in 1860, the paper predicted, would plunge the nation into a bloody civil war. Even newspapers friendly to Seward felt that his statements were impolitic and damaging to the Republican cause and needlessly provocative to the South. In the slave states, the speech played into the hands of the fire-eaters, confirming their claims that Republicans were determined to rid the South of slavery by any means, not excluding violence. Seward's language, they said, was a declaration of war against the South.[1]

What was not widely recognized at the time, however, was that Abraham Lincoln had anticipated Seward by about four months, in what has been regarded as one of the greatest speeches ever delivered. Lacking Seward's stature, Lincoln attracted little notice outside Illinois, and almost none in the slaveholding states. There was no reason to be concerned with the statements made by an "obscure abolitionist lawyer in Illinois," one Southern paper explained, for even if he should be elected to the Senate, his power to harm the South would be virtually nil. Only later, after the South discovered Lincoln, did his statements in the 1858 campaign become critical. Lincoln was then credited with having first employed the irrepressible conflict argument. Seward, it seemed, had only borrowed it from Lincoln.[2]

In fact, neither Lincoln nor Seward can claim the "honor" of having originated the argument, although they clearly deserve the credit for introducing it into sectional politics at a time when the conflict surely called for more restrained utterances. That the struggle be-

---

1. George E. Baker, ed., *The Works of William H. Seward* (5 vols.; New York and Boston, 1853–84), IV, 289–302; New York *Herald*, October 28, 29, 30, November 1, 1858; Frederic Bancroft, *The Life of William H. Seward* (2 vols.; New York, 1900), I, 458–61. Seward later remarked that "if heaven would forgive him for stringing together two high-sounding words, he would never do it again." Glyndon G. Van Deusen, *William Henry Seward* (New York, 1967), 194.

2. Milledgeville (Ga.) *Federal Union*, September 14, October 10, 1858; Donald E. Reynolds, *Editors Make War: Southern Newspapers in the Secession Crisis* (Nashville, 1970), 56–57; J. D. B. De Bow, "Presidential Candidates and Aspirants," *De Bow's Review*, XXIX (July, 1860), 102.

tween slavery and freedom was "ancient and eternal" and that the struggle would not cease until one or the other had expired had long been expressed by the abolitionists; by the 1850s, it found echoes among the defenders of slavery as well. In 1858, however, sectional antagonism, fueled by the Dred Scott decision, the Lecompton crisis, the growth of the Republican party, and the split among Democrats, had moved to a new and more explosive stage, a level of abstraction that gave the irrepressible conflict argument a dangerous volatility. Seward provided the catchy phrase, encapsulating the antislavery argument in two ominous but descriptive words, while Lincoln gave the idea a divine sanction through his clever use of a biblical metaphor. In each instance, the manner and timing of the expression enhanced its impact. The concept was absolute and uncompromising; it left no room for mediation. Not only did Lincoln and Seward inflame the controversy but they both also expressed what would become a self-fulfilling prophecy.

Following his re-entry into politics as a vigorous opponent of slavery expansion, Lincoln often skirted the notion of an irrepressible conflict, without expressing it outright. William H. Herndon, a frequently unreliable source, recalled that Lincoln believed the slavery question could "never be successfully compromised" even before he was aroused in 1854 by the repeal of the Missouri Compromise. According to his law partner, he likened slavery and freedom to two wild beasts, chained in sight of one another but held apart. "Some day," Lincoln allegedly remarked, "these deadly antagonists will one or the other break their bonds, and then the question will be settled."

One need not rely solely on Herndon's memory for evidence that Lincoln was moving toward an irrepressible conflict position before he delivered his "House Divided" speech. In the fall of 1854, he had appeared as a strong supporter of sectional compromise as the only proper and practical resolution of the slavery issue. Not only did he demand the restoration of the Missouri Compromise but he also warned that the failure to do so would "strangle and cast from us forever" that spirit of compromise that had proved so vital to the preservation of the Union. At that time, he blamed extremists in both the North and the South for inciting conflict between the sections. Lincoln's way was the middle way, the way of mutual concessions. The "grave question for the lovers of the Union," as he then put it, was whether the spirit of compromise would be allowed to continue saving the Union.

Lincoln's mood shifted following his defeat for the Senate early in 1855, when he realized that a national solution, through the agency of a revitalized Whig party, was no longer a possibility. Depressed and apparently facing an uncertain political future, he seemed to lose faith that the slavery issue could ever be settled peaceably. The contest for Kansas degenerated into a confused and bloody struggle, while the new Republican party, capitalizing on the turmoil, was growing stronger in the North. For Lincoln, the "grave question" now became, "Can we as a nation continue together *permanently— forever*—half slave and half free?" His former confidence in the spirit of compromise was lost. He had no answer to the question. The problem, he confessed, was too "mighty" for him, and he preferred to leave its resolution to a higher authority. "May God, in his mercy, superintend the solution."

Lincoln, however, decided not to wait for providential intervention, for as soon as he cast his lot with the Republican party his uncertainty disappeared. What had been too mighty a question for him in 1855, became a positive assertion and prediction in the year that followed. Echoing the abolitionists, he boldly avowed "that there could be no Union with slavery." The controversy, he said, would be "ceaseless" until slavery were "swept away." And in language not to be misunderstood, he proclaimed that "our government could not last—part slave and part free." There was no longer room for compromise. As he responded to the Dred Scott decision and the Lecompton crisis in the winter of 1857–58, Lincoln used almost the precise language he would later employ in his "House Divided" speech. The "grave question" now assumed its final arbitrary stage: "Welcome, or unwelcome, agreeable, or disagreeable, whether this shall be an entire slave nation, *is* the issue before us."[3]

3. William H. Herndon and Jesse W. Weik, *Herndon's Life of Lincoln*, ed. Paul M. Angle (Cleveland, 1949), 292, 295; Speech at Peoria, Illinois, October 16, 1854, Lincoln to George Robertson, August 15, 1855, Speech at Springfield, Illinois, June 10, 1856, Fragment of a Speech, ca. May 18, 1858 (for the proper dating of this document, see above, chap. 2, n. 27), in *The Collected Works of Abraham Lincoln*, ed. Roy P. Basler et al. (9 vols; New Brunswick, N.J., 1954), II, 272, 318, 345, 452–54. On the

Lincoln delivered his "House Divided" speech on June 16, 1858, in the statehouse in Springfield, before a cheering audience of Republican faithful. Earlier in the day, he had listened to a former congressman and friend, Richard Yates, describe the party as the most powerful on the North American continent. Lincoln was named to lead that party in the state elections as the candidate for Stephen A. Douglas' senate seat, and his speech was both an acceptance of the nomination and an effort to unite the party behind his candidacy. He was aware of the significance of the occasion to both his career and to the future of the Republican cause. Douglas had not yet left Washington; the field, for the moment, was Lincoln's alone. He knew that his remarks would not only open the campaign but that they would also provide what one paper called the "ground work" for all the speechmaking to come. For weeks he had been laboring over the themes of the speech, and as the day for delivery approached, he wrote it all out in carefully considered language in order that it could "get into print" and be available, as he said, to a public "beyond the circle of my hearers." It was to be the most important statement of his career, and he hoped that it would be circulated beyond the borders of his state.

The "House Divided" speech, in purpose and theme, sprang from the peculiar and confused political situation within which the election was to be fought, a speech, as one contemporary put it, that was "made at the commencement of a campaign and apparently made for the campaign." Eastern Republicans, impressed with Douglas' stand against the proslavery Kansas Lecompton constitution, urged the senator's re-election, and Lincoln was fearful lest rank-and-file Republicans be lured into the Douglas column. Furthermore, Douglas' split with the South and his well-publicized attack against the effort to impose slavery on Kansas threatened to put the Republicans' principal argument against the Little Giant off the track. Lincoln, aware of the difficulties that seemed to stand in his way, was undaunted. In order to discourage defections, he needed to dramatize and exaggerate the differences between Douglas and the Republicans, and one effective way to accomplish this was

---

dating of the fragment, see also Don E. Fehrenbacher, *Prelude to Greatness: Lincoln in the 1850's* (Stanford, 1962), 89–92.

by grounding the party more firmly than he had before on a foundation of moral principle. With the differences sharply drawn along moral lines, ruling out any possibility of a middle position, the irrepressibility of the conflict over slavery became a major theme in Lincoln's argument. At the same time, by identifying Douglas with the Southern slaveholding interests, he was able to charge the senator with doing the South's work to the detriment of his own section's interests. That Douglas had split with the Southern leadership over Lecompton did not deter Lincoln, for he argued that the quarrel was not really with the South at all but was simply a squabble between the senator and the president, not to be taken seriously.[4]

The "House Divided " speech was so important to Lincoln that he rehearsed it, first before his law partner and then before a group of a dozen or more Republican friends. Herndon was delighted with what he heard. It was "compact—nervous—eloquent," the best expression "of the ideas of . . . Republicanism" he had seen or heard. He complained mildly that the speech seemed too conservative, but agreed that since it was a political statement its prudence was appropriate. Lincoln's friends had an opposite reaction. It was a "d——d fool utterance," said one, too radical in its sentiments. Another warned that Lincoln's remarks were "too far in advance of the times." Lincoln was not swayed; he was determined to deliver the speech precisely as he had written it.[5]

Most of Lincoln's speech was devoted to a review of Douglas' relations with President Buchanan, and to a self-serving analysis of Douglas' position that even the Little Giant had trouble recognizing. Although Lincoln denied any intention to misrepresent Douglas or to question his motives, he managed to do a good job of it nonetheless. The points he impressed upon the Republicans were, first, that the rift between Douglas on the one hand, and Buchanan and the

4. Springfield *Illinois State Journal*, June 25, 1858; Speech at Columbus, Ohio, September 16, 1859, in *Collected Works*, III, 406; Leonard Swett to William H. Herndon, July 17, 1866, in Emanuel Hertz, *The Hidden Lincoln: From the Letters and Papers of William H. Herndon* (New York, 1938), 296; "A House Divided": Speech at Springfield, Illinois, June 16, 1858, in *Collected Works*, II, 463.

5. David Donald, *Lincoln's Herndon* (New York, 1948), 118–19. Years later, Herndon recalled that after each member of the group had criticized the speech, he said: "Lincoln, deliver that speech as read and it will make you President." Herndon and Weik, *Herndon's Life of Lincoln*, 326.

South on the other, was of no real importance; and, second, that Douglas had not altered his position toward the extension of slavery since he had repealed the Missouri Compromise in the Kansas-Nebraska Act. Lincoln warned party members not to make too much of Douglas' struggle against the Lecompton constitution, in which he had received Republican support, for it was focused solely on the "right of a people to make their own constitution," a point on which Douglas and the Republicans had never differed. What did matter, Lincoln declared, in a deliberate distortion of Douglas' meaning, was Douglas' insistence that "he cares not whether slavery be voted *down* or voted *up*"; this was the policy the senator wished to impress upon the public mind. Indeed, after the Dred Scott decision's demolition of popular sovereignty, it was the "only shred left of his original Nebraska doctrine."

But, it seemed, Douglas did care after all whether slavery was voted up or down, for Lincoln went on to charge the senator with conspiring to extend slavery throughout the free states of the North. Although he hedged his accusation with the admission that he could not know for sure, he nonetheless maintained that Douglas, Chief Justice Roger B. Taney, and Presidents Pierce and Buchanan had formed a conspiracy to nationalize slavery. The four men, he alleged, had "worked upon a common plan or draft" for extending slavery throughout the United States even before the Kansas-Nebraska Act was passed. Lincoln offered no evidence to support the charge; instead he offered an analogy to demonstrate its validity—the four workmen, Stephen, Franklin, Roger, and James, joining "a lot of framed timbers" to make a house or a mill, "all the tenons and mortices exactly fitting, and all the lengths and proportions of the different pieces exactly adapted to their respective places." It was precisely the kind of analogy his audience could appreciate.

Once begun, the momentum of accusation was accelerated. Douglas, Lincoln pointed out, had labored for years "to prove it a sacred right of white men to take negro slaves into the new Territories." The states were next, he warned, for "we may, ere long, see . . . another Supreme Court decision, declaring that the Constitution of the United States does not permit a *State* to exclude slavery from its limits." And, Lincoln inferred, Douglas was bound to declare his support of the revival of the African slave trade. How could any Republican, in good faith and conscience, back such a man?

Lincoln did not mince his words. With his charges against the senator echoing through the minds of his audience, he closed with a stern lecture to all party members to remain steadfast, to resist the blandishments of the Democrats, and to support the Republican ticket with all the vigor they could muster. Douglas, he reminded them, "is not now with us—he does not pretend to be—he does not promise to ever be." Stand firm, and "we *shall not fail.*"[6]

It was neither Lincoln's barrage of charges against Douglas nor his plea for party unity that aroused misgivings among some of his Republican friends. Rather, it was the statement with which he opened his speech, a series of pointed assertions designed, in their brevity, simplicity, and directness, to hit hard at his audience's emotions. Lincoln had carefully measured the impact of his language so that it would reach beyond the confines of the hall in which he spoke and would influence the thinking of Republicans throughout the North. He intended, he told Herndon, to use some "universally known figure expressed in simple language" that would "strike home to the minds of men in order to raise them up to the peril of the times." Lincoln, it seems clear, was looking beyond the legislative elections that would determine the choice of United States senator, and beyond the voters in Illinois, but whether or not he aspired to anything more than a place in his party's leadership is problematical.

Lincoln began with a reminder that the agitation over slavery had intensified rather than abated since the passage of the Kansas-Nebraska Act, contrary to the "avowed object, and confident promise" of the legislation. Implying that the responsibility for the Act's failure to end the agitation belonged to its supporters rather than to its opponents, Lincoln gravely prophesied that the agitation would not cease, but would continue "until a crisis shall have been reached and passed." To emphasize the inevitability of the crisis, he em-

6. Robert W. Johannsen, ed., *The Lincoln-Douglas Debates of 1858* (New York, 1965), 16–18, 19, 20–21. These and all subsequent quotations from the "House Divided" speech have been taken from the text in this edition, which differs in some respects from that in the *Collected Works*. For a discussion of the differences, see Don E. Fehrenbacher, "The Words of Lincoln," in Fehrenbacher, *Lincoln in Text and Context: Collected Essays* (Stanford, 1987), 275–77.

ployed a well-known biblical metaphor, a paraphrase of the words of Jesus Christ:

"A house divided against itself cannot stand." I believe this government cannot endure permanently half slave and half free. I do not expect the Union to be dissolved—I do not expect the house to fall—but I do expect it will cease to be divided. It will become all one thing, or all the other. Either the opponents of slavery will arrest the further spread of it, and place it where the public mind shall rest in the belief that it is in the course of ultimate extinction; or its advocates will push it forward, till it shall become alike lawful in all the States, old as well as new—North as well as South.

With these few lines, which have assumed mystical, even mythical qualities in the Lincoln canon, Lincoln tied the abolition of slavery to the notion of irrepressible conflict, thereby pushing the agitation over slavery to a new extreme.[7]

Lincoln offered no clues as to the nature of the crisis which he anticipated; nor did he suggest the means by which slavery would either be abolished in the South or legalized in the North. While he would later speak of the "ultimate peaceable extinction" of slavery, his use of the irrepressible conflict (or inevitable crisis) idea seemed to rule out a peaceful resolution of the slavery issue. By assuming the moralistic tone of the abolitionists and grounding his position on divine authority, he added a new dimension to the sectional conflict that could only result in a further polarization on the slavery issue. His opening expression in the "House Divided" speech, Lincoln said, was a "truth of all human experience"; it had been true "for six thousand years." There was to be no backing away from it. "I would rather be defeated with this expression in the speech," Herndon recalled Lincoln saying, "and uphold and discuss it before the people, than be victorious without it." Even if one takes into account Herndon's tendency toward embellishment, Lincoln nonetheless appeared resolute in his determination to stand by his speech.[8]

7. Herndon and Weik, *Herndon's Life of Lincoln*, 325; Johannsen, ed., *The Lincoln-Douglas Debates of 1858*, 14. The biblical verse is from Mark 3:25: "And if an house be divided against itself, that house cannot stand" (King James Version).

8. Speech at Edwardsville, Illinois, September 11, 1858, in *Collected Works*, III, 93; Herndon and Weik, *Herndon's Life of Lincoln*, 325. Not only did the opening statement of the "House Divided" speech provide Lincoln with a platform for the 1858 election, but it also remained the centerpiece of his position in subsequent years. He reaffirmed its sentiments on numerous occasions during the 1860 presidential election

Douglas quickly learned that he faced a formidable combination. When he challenged the appropriateness of the "house divided" metaphor, Lincoln responded by referring him to a higher source, pointing out that Douglas' quarrel was not with him but with the Saviour. If Douglas thought that a "house divided against itself *can stand*," Lincoln contended, "then there is a question of veracity . . . between the Judge and an authority of a somewhat higher character." Later, feeling less charitable toward his opponent, Lincoln compared Douglas' attack on his "house divided" proposition with Satan's war on the Bible. Still, Douglas persisted, questioning the applicability of the "language of our Lord" to the "American Union and American constitution." When did Lincoln learn, he asked, "and by what authority does he proclaim, that this government is contrary to the law of God, and cannot stand?" For Lincoln, however, there was no debate. The maxim "put forth by the Saviour" was beyond question. "Certainly," he observed, "there is no contending against the Will of God." It was a lesson, apparently, that Douglas had yet to learn.[9]

When Lincoln adapted the "house divided" metaphor to the politics of the sectional conflict, he was employing a favorite rhetorical device in early nineteenth-century political discourse. It had become so common by the late 1850s that one historian has labeled it "almost a cliché." Abolitionists had used it to promote immediate emancipation, Daniel Webster used it on behalf of the Union, and even

and during the secession crisis that followed. For Southerners, it became the "true issue" that separated them from the North and was cited as justification for secession. See, for example, Lincoln to Oliver P. Hall, Jacob N. Fullinwider, and William F. Correll, February 14, 1860, in *Collected Works*, III, 519–20; Charles M. Segal, ed., *Conversations with Lincoln* (New York, 1961), 86; Charleston *Mercury*, August 4, 1860; and *De Bow's Review*, XXIX (December, 1860), 798.

9. First Debate with Stephen A. Douglas at Ottawa, Illinois, August 21, 1858, Seventh and Last Debate with Stephen A. Douglas at Alton, Illinois, October 15, 1858, Third Debate with Stephen A. Douglas at Jonesboro, Illinois, September 15, 1858 (Douglas' Speech), Fragment on Pro-Slavery Theology, October 1, 1858?, in *Collected Works*, III, 17, 305, 111, 204. Lincoln had earlier equated the Republican position with that of "the God of the right," and later declared, in a statement to delegates to the Washington Peace Conference in February, 1861, that "freedom is the natural condition of the human race, in which the Almighty intended men to live. Those who fight the purposes of the Almighty will not succeed. They always have been, they always will be, beaten." Lincoln to Charles D. Gilfillan, May 9, 1857, in *Collected Works*, II, 395; Segal, ed., *Conversations with Lincoln*, 84.

secessionists had used it to justify disunion. Lincoln himself cited it when he appealed for Whig party unity as far back as 1843.[10]

Furthermore, Lincoln borrowed his prediction that the country would become "all one thing, or all the other" from the South's controversial apologist for slavery, the Virginian George Fitzhugh (although the concept too had been a stock element for many years in both proslavery and antislavery arguments). If Herndon can be believed, Lincoln read Fitzhugh's classic defense of slavery, *Sociology for the South; or, The Failure of Free Society*, soon after it appeared in 1854, and was aroused to anger. He included veiled references to Fitzhugh's argument in his Peoria Speech that fall, assuming (erroneously) that its aggressive proslavery defense accurately reflected Southern opinion. Since 1854, Lincoln's statements had often been sprinkled with Fitzhugh's assertions, derived from unsigned editorials in the Richmond *Enquirer.* It proved to be good campaign material with which to frighten Northern, especially Illinois, voters. Because the *Enquirer* supported Douglas in the senatorial contest, Lincoln was able to fasten Fitzhugh's extreme position on his opponent, while the Republican press reprinted the arguments with alarming and fearful headlines linking Douglas to Southern fire-eaters.[11]

Thus armed with the authority of Scripture and George Fitzhugh, Lincoln sallied forth in defense of freedom, to do combat with Douglas and the forces of moral darkness the senator represented. The campaign assumed the characteristics of a crusade, as Lincoln described with a heightened intensity the wide moral gulf that separated Republicans from the Little Giant. The irrepressible conflict—the inevitability of crisis and the futility of sectional conciliation—became in its effect a new higher law in the struggle. The

10. Fehrenbacher, *Prelude to Greatness,* 183 n. 45; Albert J. Beveridge, *Abraham Lincoln, 1809–1858* (2 vols.; Boston, 1928), II, 575 n. 2; Campaign Circular from Whig Committee, March 4, 1843, in *Collected Works,* I, 315.

11. Herndon and Weik, *Herndon's Life of Lincoln,* 293; Herndon to Weik, October 28, 1885, in Hertz, *The Hidden Lincoln,* 96–97; Harvey Wish, *George Fitzhugh: Propagandist of the Old South* (Baton Rouge, 1943), 150–56; Chicago *Press and Tribune,* July 31, 1858. Lincoln should have known (if he was the reader recent writers have claimed him to be) that Southerners themselves rejected Fitzhugh's extreme arguments. See "Failure of Free Societies," *Southern Literary Messenger,* XXI (March, 1855), 129–41.

"House Divided" speech, considered by modern historians as the "most provocative utterance" of Lincoln's career and his "most radical pronouncement" on the slavery issue, was noted in the Eastern press even before Douglas left the national capital, fulfilling Lincoln's wish that his statement would reach beyond the Illinois borders. The New York *Tribune* printed the speech in full. Calling it "compact and forcible" and a "concise and admirable statement," Horace Greeley noted that "Mr. Lincoln never fails to make a good speech, when he makes any, and this is one of his best efforts." In contrast, the New York *Herald* charged that the speech placed Lincoln "on the high road, with Lloyd Garrison and all the ungodly abolition crew, to bloody revolution, disunion, anarchy, and all the horrors of an endless war of sections." Two years later, the *Herald* credited Lincoln with "oracular language" when he proclaimed the irrepressible conflict, for it had now become the "mission of the prophet himself to fulfill" the prediction.[12]

Douglas was alarmed at the direction Lincoln gave to the 1858 campaign. The issues between them, Douglas proclaimed, were "direct, unequivocal, and irreconcilable." Lincoln's "house divided" statement and the "all one thing or all the other" doctrine raised serious questions about the nature of the republic, and placed the Union in unwonted peril. Lincoln's predictions, he believed, were equivalent to a call for war between the sections, for he could not conceive how "all the states shall either become free or become slave" without some violent upheaval. More familiar than Lincoln with Southern attitudes and concerns from his years of political association with Southerners, Douglas could conceive of no contingency by which slavery would be eliminated in the states without violence; nor could he believe that slavery would ever be spread throughout the Northern free states by peaceful means. Yet this was what Lincoln seemed to be arguing. Douglas concluded that Lin-

---

12. Fehrenbacher, *Prelude to Greatness*, 71; Mark E. Neely, Jr., *The Abraham Lincoln Encyclopedia* (New York, 1982), 152; New York *Tribune*, June 24, 1858; New York *Herald*, July 14, 1858, June 2, 1860. In the South, Lincoln's "House Divided" speech caused scarcely a ripple; it was discovered by Southern editors only after Lincoln was unexpectedly nominated for the presidency in 1860, when one Southern spokesman charged that Lincoln was the "real author of the higher law and irrepressible conflict," for they were "but part and parcel of each other." *De Bow's Review*, XXIX (December, 1860), 798.

coln's forecast simply revealed a woeful lack of understanding of slavery, the South, and of the Southern temperament.

But, Douglas feared, Lincoln did not only misunderstand the South. He had also "totally misapprehended the great principle upon which our government rests." His effort to impose on the nation a uniformity of local laws and institutions and a moral homogeneity dictated by the central government, Douglas believed, placed at defiance the intentions of the republic's founders. It was the contest all over again between the "one consolidated empire" of the Federalists and Whigs, and the "confederacy of sovereign and equal states" of Jefferson and Jackson. When Lincoln went further and wrapped his commitment to consolidation in the cloak of moral principle and invoked Holy Scripture on its behalf, thereby implying that his opponents were both immoral and un-Christian, he struck a blow against all those safeguards "which our institutions have thrown around the rights of the citizens," a blow that might well prove fatal to the republic itself. "Uniformity," Douglas warned, "is the parent of despotism the world over, not only in politics, but in religion."[13]

But, Lincoln protested, that was not his intention at all. Furthermore, he was surprised that anyone could so misconstrue his words as to suggest that he would ever support interference with slavery in the states where it existed. Yet to Douglas that was a logical inference from the language of the "House Divided" speech. Douglas' attacks on the speech, repeated throughout the campaign, forced Lincoln to explain his meaning over and over again. With each explanation, Douglas felt, the ambivalence of Lincoln's position became more apparent. Lincoln denied that he had proposed a war between the sections, and that he had ever contemplated the ultimate extinction of slavery by force. The idea of "forcing slavery into a free State, or out of a slave State, at the point of a bayonet," he declared, was nonsense. "Not *bloody bullets*," Lincoln had explained, "but *peaceful ballots* only, are necessary. . . . It only needs that every right thinking man, shall go to the polls, and without fear or prejudice, *vote* as he *thinks*." It did not require a great leap of imagination

13. Speech of Stephen A. Douglas, Chicago, July 9, 1858, in Johannsen, ed., *The Lincoln-Douglas Debates of 1858*, 29–30, 34.

to conclude that Lincoln's "right thinking man" was one who supported the Republican position on the slavery question.

If Douglas found Lincoln hard to pin down, it was because Lincoln had put forth a "proposition so broad in its abolitionism as to cover the whole ground." Why, Douglas asked, did not Lincoln pledge to vote, as senator, against the admission of another slave state, if he really believed that the Union could not endure half-slave and half-free? While Lincoln reaffirmed his belief that the government could not endure permanently half-slave and half-free, he also suggested that the admission of one more slave state would hardly "permanently fix the character and establish this as a universal slave nation." Clearly, Lincoln felt, the divided house could indeed endure for a very long time.[14]

Still, Douglas persisted, and Lincoln became more impatient as he became more defensive. With each response, he seemed to weaken the impact of his "house divided" statement, to rob it of its immediacy. "I only said what I expected would take place," he explained. "I made a prediction only—it may have been a foolish one perhaps." He later confided that he meant to express only an "abstract opinion" and never intended that it should be the basis for political action. He lashed back at Douglas for "working up these quibbles," but Douglas felt that the situation was too critical for Lincoln to dismiss the questions raised by his speech as mere quibbles over words. The issue, he believed, lay at the heart of the conflict over slavery and involved the "perpetuity of the Union" and the "peace and harmony of the different sections of the republic." Lincoln's expression was the "fatal heresy" that threatened to bring down the republic.

In a rare display of "fairness" toward Douglas, Lincoln remarked

14. Speech at Chicago, Illinois, July 10, 1858, Fragment: Notes for Speeches, ca. August 21, 1858, Fragment of a Speech, ca. May 18, 1858, Second Debate with Stephen A. Douglas at Freeport, Illinois, August 27, 1858, in *Collected Works*, II, 492, 551, 454, III, 67 (Douglas' speech), 73. When Lincoln was asked to explain the meaning of his "House Divided" speech to his friends, he confessed that he was "much mortified that any part of it should be construed so differently from any thing intended by me." He had not dreamed that his language could be taken to suggest "any power or purpose, to interfere with slavery in the States where it exists." Whether the words "bear such construction or not, I never so intended it." Lincoln to John L. Scripps, June 23, 1858, in *Collected Works*, II, 471.

that "if he thinks I am doing something which leads to these bad results, it is none the better that I did not mean it." The consequence would be "just as fatal to the country . . . whether I intend it or not." In a familiar, but less than convincing tone, Lincoln pleaded that he was not a "master of language," had no "fine education," and was "not capable of entering into a disquisition upon dialectics." But, he insisted, "I know what I meant." [15]

In his last public appearance before the 1858 election, Lincoln reviewed the campaign and asked his friends for sympathetic understanding. Speaking in a calm and subdued manner, in language filled with humility, he stated that he had never intended to attack the motives of any party or individual, but had himself been charged repeatedly with trying to destroy the Union. "Bespattered with every imaginable odious epithet," he had nonetheless "cultivated patience, and made no attempt at a retort." The experience, he confessed, had been a "painful" one for him. "To the best of my judgment," he asserted, "I have labored *for*, and not *against* the Union." In words that recalled his Peoria Speech four years before, Lincoln extended the hand of friendship to the South. He had always been careful, he said, to avoid any "harsh sentiment towards our Southern brethren." The only difference "between them and us, is the difference of circumstances." In an appeal to the conservative wing of his party, he reminded his audience that he had "neither assailed, nor wrestled with" any portion of the Constitution, had upheld the legal right of Southerners to reclaim their fugitives, and had denied the legal right of Congress to interfere with slavery in the states. All he desired was simply the restoration of the Missouri Compromise, the toleration of slavery "by *necessity*" where it existed, and "unyielding hostility" to the extension of slavery, "on principle." Noticeably absent from his summary was any trace of the doctrines he had propounded in his "House Divided" speech. [16]

15. Speech at Chicago, Illinois, July 10, 1858, *Collected Works*, II, 491; Segal, ed., *Conversations with Lincoln*, 86; New York *Herald*, December 6, 1858 (Douglas' speech at Memphis, November 29, 1858); First Debate with Stephen A. Douglas at Ottawa, Illinois, August 21, 1858, in *Collected Works*, III, 19.

16. Fragment: Last Speech of the Campaign at Springfield, Illinois, October 30, 1858, in *Collected Works*, III, 334. Lincoln also seemed to disclaim any political ambition. Although ambition had been "ascribed to me," he remarked, "God knows how sincerely I prayed from the first that this field of ambition might not be opened." Was

In spite of this last-minute effort to downplay his irrepressible conflict doctrine, he continued to stand behind it in his private correspondence. When Seward delivered what Douglas suggested was merely his version of Lincoln's platform, Lincoln was heartened that the idea was "attracting more and more attention." Seward, he was certain, had not "uttered that sentiment because I had done so before" but had done so because he "saw the truth of it." "You see," he told an Ohio gathering, "we are multiplying." [17]

Lincoln did not win the 1858 election against Douglas, and some Republicans blamed his "House Divided" speech for his defeat. To one supporter, his language had sounded too much like "an implied pledge on behalf of the Republican party to make war upon the institution of slavery in the States where it now exists." Another commented that Lincoln was defeated by the "first ten lines of the first speech he made" in the campaign. While Lincoln expressed his disappointment with the election result, he stood by the position he had taken. He knew that "some very good people" had commented unfavorably on something he had said, or was supposed to have said, during the campaign, and perhaps even withheld their support because of it. In the future, he hoped that individuals who agreed that slavery was a moral, political, and social wrong, and therefore ought to be treated as a wrong, would not allow "anything minor or subsidiary" to dissuade them from supporting the party. "You may think that speech was a mistake," he told a group of Republicans, "but I never have believed it was, and you will see the day when you will consider it was the wisest thing I ever said." Lincoln has proved to be a good prophet, perhaps better than he had any reason to believe. [18]

If Lincoln had failed in his own race, he was satisfied that he had saved the Republican party, not just in Illinois but in the nation at

---

he saying that he had not sought and did not want the senate seat for which he had campaigned?

17. New York *Herald*, December 6, 1858; Speech at Columbus, Ohio, September 16, 1859, in *Collected Works*, III, 408.

18. John L. Scripps to Lincoln, June 22, 1858, in Abraham Lincoln Papers, Library of Congress (microfilm); Leonard Swett to Herndon, July 17, 1866, in Hertz, *The Hidden Lincoln*, 296; Speech at Chicago, Illinois, March 1, 1859, in *Collected Works*, III, 366.

large. If Illinois Republicans had made Douglas their candidate as some outside the state had urged, Lincoln maintained early in 1859, "there would to-day be no Republican party in this Union." All the effort that had gone into building the party would have been "entirely lost." He reminded party members of what he hoped they had come to realize: dally with Douglas, fall in behind him, and "they do not absorb him, he absorbs them." They would, he was certain, "come out at the end all Douglas men." Lincoln felt that he had forestalled disaster for his party and for his own political prospects. Indeed, he emerged from the campaign with a strengthened reputation, both within and outside his state. Following the election, Horace Greeley's New York *Tribune* hailed Lincoln's campaign speeches as pungent and powerful, and his "House Divided" speech as a "condensed statement of the issues which divide the Republicans from the Democrats" that has "rarely or never been exceeded." No man, the paper concluded, could have "upborne the Republican standard more gallantly." [19]

Complementing Lincoln's irrepressible conflict doctrine, its "twin," so to speak, was the Slave Power conspiracy charge, probably the most effective weapon against his longtime adversary that he had in his political arsenal. To Lincoln, Douglas was the personification of the Southern slave interest, anxious to further its influence and power, outdoing even the Southerners in his zeal. He was not only one of the conspirators, he was their ringleader. That Lincoln should have invested so much of his time and ingenuity to the Slave Power conspiracy argument was not surprising, for as David Brion Davis has shown, conspiratorial imagery was a "formalized staple" in the political discourse of the sectional conflict. Abolitionists had long employed it, with good effect, and it was adopted early by the political antislavery movement. By the mid-1850s, it had become the "master symbol of the Republican party." [20]

19. Speech at Chicago, Illinois, March 1, 1859, in *Collected Works*, III, 367; New York *Tribune*, November 17, 1858.

20. David Brion Davis, *The Slave Power Conspiracy and the Paranoid Style* (Baton Rouge, 1969), 7 and *passim*; William E. Gienapp, "The Republican Party and the Slave Power," in *New Perspectives on Race and Slavery in America: Essays in Honor of Kenneth M. Stampp*, ed. Robert H. Abzug and Stephen A. Maizlish (Lexington, 1986), 53.

The conspiracy charge offered Lincoln a neat, simplistic, and emotionally charged stratagem for persuading Republicans of the great gulf that separated them from Douglas, for convincing the voters that slavery was a serious threat to free society in the Northern states, and for branding his opponent as a dangerous and devious plotter bent on subverting the republic. Lincoln's charge gained credibility from the momentum of the conflict. The Fugitive Slave Act, the Kansas-Nebraska Act, the Dred Scott decision, the violence in Kansas, and the Lecompton constitution all appeared to Lincoln as interconnected parts of a single whole, from which he inferred some organized effort on the part of an aggressive slavocracy in which the Little Giant was a prime mover. Obviously, the South could not have won these measures without some secret and carefully planned conspiracy. In identifying the conspirators, Lincoln carefully separated the Slave Power from the Southern people, enabling him to plead (as he still did on occasion) that he harbored no grievance against them. Of the four conspirators named by Lincoln, three were Northern Democrats—Franklin Pierce, James Buchanan, and Douglas; the fourth, Chief Justice Roger B. Taney, was a Southerner and a slaveholder, but he hailed from a border state.

As he urged Republicans to resist the lure of Douglas, Lincoln argued with all the confidence of one who was privy to secret information that control of the territories would hardly satisfy the insatiable appetite of the Slave Power, and that the extension of slavery into Kansas and Nebraska was but a first step toward spreading the institution throughout the free states. The goal of Douglas and his fellow conspirators, he charged, was to convert the republic into a vast slave empire. Another Supreme Court decision that would make slavery lawful in all the states, he announced, was "probably coming" and would "soon be upon us" unless the present political "dynasty" of Douglas and the Democrats were overthrown. "We shall lie down pleasantly dreaming that the people of Missouri are on the verge of making their State free, and we shall awake to the reality instead, that the Supreme Court had made Illinois a slave State." Powerful language, with just enough credibility to frighten wavering Republicans. [21]

21. Johannsen, ed., *The Lincoln-Douglas Debates of 1858*, 19–20.

As Lincoln honed the conspiracy charge against Douglas to a fine edge, he simply made more explicit a tactic that had been employed against Douglas for years by Whigs and Republicans. He had been painted in dark, sinister colors from the moment the slavery issue had surfaced in the politics of the 1840s. When Douglas supported the annexation of Texas and the war with Mexico, he was described as the "most servile tool that has crawled in the slime and scum of slavery at the foot of the slave power." When he spoke out against the Wilmot Proviso, he was a "dough-faced renegade" who should be "branded with the mark of Cain," and his support for Lewis Cass in the 1848 presidential race was regarded as proof of his "disgraceful servility to the slave influence." On the Missouri Compromise, Douglas could not be right, no matter which side he took. When he defended the Compromise and urged that it be extended to the Pacific Ocean, he was denounced as "willing to gratify the south in their cherished desire of forming more Slave States"; several years later, when he repealed the Compromise, he was accused by the same voices of promoting an "atrocious plot" to convert the free West into a "dreary region of despotism." Douglas was "down on his marrow-bones" at the "feet of slavery." [22]

Little wonder, then, that Douglas ignored Lincoln's charge that he was the leader of a Slave Power conspiracy. He had heard it all before. His silence, however, was short-lived, for Lincoln seized upon his lack of complaint as an admission of guilt, proving the accusation to be true. His "House Divided" speech, he said, had been delivered "with the most kindly feeling towards Judge Douglas." He made no inferences that did not appear to be true. "I planted myself upon the truth, and the truth only, so far as I knew it." Because Douglas had not complained of being misrepresented, obviously all that had been said of him was correct. The *Illinois State Journal* supported Lincoln's conclusion: Although the charge had been pressed "time and again," Douglas always "sneaks away from the issue."

When Douglas finally did respond, he denounced Lincoln's accusation as an "infamous lie" and an outrageous attack on his moral

22. The quotations are from Robert W. Johannsen, "Stephen A. Douglas and the South," in Johannsen, *The Frontier, the Union, and Stephen A. Douglas* (Urbana, 1989), 187–88.

integrity. "I did not answer the charge before," he explained, "for the reason that I did not suppose there was a man in America with a heart so corrupt as to believe such a charge could be true."[23]

Lincoln shrugged off Douglas' denial with the simple retort, "What of it?" It did not disturb the "facts in evidence"; it only made Douglas the "dupe, instead of a principal, of conspirators." But Lincoln was too smart a politician not to leave open a path for retreat. He made the charge, he said, because he believed that the evidence of a "thousand corroborating circumstances" bore him out; but, he pleaded, he had never pretended to have personal knowledge of Douglas' involvement in a conspiracy. Furthermore, he added, he did not wish to suggest that Douglas "means it so" when he prepares the way for making slavery national, implying that Douglas was an unwitting participant in the proslavery movement. Finally, Lincoln suggested the possibility that there was no conspiracy at all. "I have not affirmed that a conspiracy does exist," he explained. "I have only stated the evidence, and affirmed my belief in its existence." When pressed, Lincoln selected his words with care. In spite of his disclaimers, however, he refused to withdraw the charge; he would not do so, he stated, until it was either proved false or until a "reasonable man" should believe it untrue, neither of which he expected.

Lincoln could not concede what many Republicans were saying, that instead of conspiring to spread slavery Douglas was trying to keep it from spreading; nor could Lincoln recognize that at the moment he made his conspiracy charge, the Southern press was attacking Douglas for conspiring with abolitionists to contain slavery. But what Lincoln could not publicly acknowledge, he privately admitted. Douglas, he wrote in the midst of the 1858 campaign, "cares nothing about the south. He knows he is already dead there."[24]

If Douglas' purpose was to nationalize slavery, as Lincoln

23. Speech at Springfield, Illinois, July 17, 1858, First Debate with Stephen A. Douglas at Ottawa, Illinois, August 21, 1858, in *Collected Works*, II, 512, III, 24 (quoting Douglas' speech at Clinton, Illinois); Springfield *Illinois State Journal*, July 27, 1858.

24. Fragment: Notes for Speeches, ca. August 21, 1858, Speech at Clinton, Illinois, July 27, 1858, Fifth Debate with Stephen A. Douglas at Galesburg, Illinois, October 7, 1858, Sixth Debate with Stephen A. Douglas at Quincy, Illinois, October 13, 1858, Lincoln to Henry Asbury, July 31, 1858, in *Collected Works*, II, 550, 525, III, 233, 282, II, 530.

claimed, popular sovereignty was his means. Popular sovereignty was the key to slavery's expansion, and Lincoln and the Republicans heaped all their deepest fears and direst warnings upon it. Horace Greeley called it a "juggle, a phantasy, a gross delusion." To Lincoln, it was nothing more than a "deceitful pretense for the benefit of slavery." He employed his best doomsday rhetoric to alarm his audiences: If popular sovereignty should prevail, he proclaimed, public opinion "will be ready for Jeff. Davis and Stephens and other leaders of that company, to sound the bugle for the revival of the slave trade, for the second Dred Scott decision, for the flood of slavery to be poured over the free States, while we shall be here tied down and helpless and run over like sheep." Few Republicans could match the quality of Lincoln's apocalyptic prophecy. But Jefferson Davis was as little enamored with popular sovereignty as was Lincoln, for the South's leaders saw in it the means for restricting and ultimately abolishing slavery. Popular sovereignty, declared Davis from the senate floor, was a "siren's song . . . a thing shadowy and fleeting, changing its color as often as the chameleon . . . a delusive gauze thrown over the public mind." It was not the South that threatened the Republican position. "It is only the insidious position of Douglas," said Lincoln, "that endangers our cause." [25]

Popular sovereignty to Douglas was simple and uncomplicated, in keeping with the American tradition of democracy and local self-government. As he defined it so many times, it meant only "that the people of each State and each territory shall be perfectly free to decide for themselves what shall be the nature and character of their institutions." Its simplicity was a major part of its appeal, and a principal reason why Douglas' opponents felt obliged to twist it into something sinister and dangerous. Popular sovereignty, worried Greeley, sounded too plausible. It "naturally commends itself to the thoughtless many who regard slaveholding as a question of convenience and profit merely. . . . 'What can be fairer,' they triumphantly ask, 'than to let each territory decide for itself − whether to

25. New York *Tribune*, November 17, 1858; Speech at Springfield, Illinois, June 26, 1857, Speech at Columbus, Ohio, September 16, 1859, Notes for Speeches at Columbus and Cincinnati, Ohio, September 16, 17, 1859, in *Collected Works*, II, 399, III, 422, 429; Jefferson Davis, quoted in Robert W. Johannsen, *Stephen A. Douglas* (New York, 1973), 695.

uphold or reject Slavery?'" In its deceptive simplicity, Lincoln called popular sovereignty "the most errant humbug that has ever been attempted on an intelligent community." However, even Lincoln himself accepted certain features of Douglas' doctrine, for example, the right of the people of a territory to make their own state constitution, even a slave state constitution if they wished, and the right of the people in the District of Columbia to prevent the abolition of slavery if they should desire to maintain the institution. Furthermore, his objection to popular sovereignty did not extend to what he called "minor domestic matters." When speaking of popular sovereignty, he said, "I wish to be understood as applying what I say to the question of slavery only." Yet even here, when Lincoln appealed to voters to elect Republicans so that slavery might be restricted, he was asking them to exercise their popular sovereignty. The decision on the moral question was, in the end, to be a political decision. Lincoln, moreover, often clouded his attacks on Douglas' doctrine with racial arguments, insisting that the territories be reserved for "free white people" and charging that popular sovereignty would surely lead in the long run to "negro equality."

In spite of Lincoln's dire forecasts, some Republicans were bothered by his ambivalence on popular sovereignty. He did not hit hard enough at Douglas' doctrine, they said, and paid too little attention to "the single point on which Mr. Douglas is strong with the unreflecting and undiscerning." Lincoln's speeches fell short of the "demolition of Mr. Douglas's castle." He should have adhered more rigidly to the "Napoleonic rule of warfare—to be stronger if possible on the point where the fortunes of the day [were] to be decided, even at the cost of being deplorably weaker, if needful, everywhere else." [26]

The differences between Lincoln and Douglas over the meaning of popular sovereignty may be better understood when placed

26. Fifth Debate with Stephen A. Douglas at Galesburg, Illinois, October 7, 1858, Speech at Springfield, Illinois, July 17, 1858, Seventh Debate with Stephen A. Douglas at Alton, Illinois, October 15, 1858, Speech at Carlinville, Illinois, August 31, 1858, in *Collected Works*, III, 218 (Douglas' Speech), II, 508–509, III, 312, 78; New York *Tribune*, November 17, 1858. At Carlinville, Lincoln warned that if Buchanan and Douglas prevailed, "negro equality will be abundant, as every white laborer will have occasion to regret when he is elbowed from his plow or his anvil by slave niggers."

within the perspective of early nineteenth-century political development. For Douglas, popular sovereignty expressed his almost transcendental faith in the popular will, his conviction that local self-government was the cornerstone of American democracy, and his belief that the strength of the Union lay precisely in its diversity. He was optimistic that if given the opportunity in a free and fair manner, the people of a territory (or of a state) would make the right decision. He stated over and over again, on the floor of the Senate and from the campaign platform, that the "people would decide against slavery if left to settle the question for themselves," as indeed they ultimately did in Kansas.

Lincoln, on the other hand, did not share Douglas' positive view of human nature and found Douglas' faith in the virtue of the people to be misplaced. From the earliest moment in his career, he had expressed a distrust of popular democracy. The keys to participation in the governance of the republic, he held, were property and intelligence; these, in turn, produced that order and stability that were so important to the functioning of a republic. An avowed enemy of what he called the "mobocratic" spirit of Jacksonian democracy, he argued instead for government by the country's "best citizens," men of property and education who had a reverence for (and a stake in) law and order. Lincoln was a republican, but not a democrat (the lowercase letters are important). In Douglas' popular sovereignty, he saw the shadow of Jackson's mass democracy. Leave the slavery question to the people to decide, he seemed to say, and the people will decide for slavery. "There are individual men in all the free states," Lincoln declared, "who desire to have slaves." Slavery, he had said, was "founded in the selfishness of man's nature." Swayed by their basest instincts, the people, if given the opportunity, would choose to perpetuate a wrong rather than to seek the right. It was a dismal view of the human character that seemed out of step with the spirit of the times. As one Lincoln supporter exclaimed, popular sovereignty was "nothing more nor less than *Mob Law.*" [27]

27. Douglas to Charles H. Lanphier, January 7, 1850, in Robert W. Johannsen, ed., *The Letters of Stephen A. Douglas* (Urbana, 1961), 182; Johannsen, "Lincoln, Liberty, and Equality," in Johannsen, *The Frontier, the Union, and Stephen A. Douglas,* 252–54; Notes for Speeches at Columbus and Cincinnati, Ohio, September 16, 17, 1859, in *Collected Works,* III, 430; Chicago *Press and Tribune,* September 3, 1858.

Douglas questioned Lincoln's insistence that the power to deal with moral issues resided exclusively with the national government, and he regarded Lincoln's interjection of moral absolutes into political discussion as dangerously divisive. The government, Lincoln explained, cannot redress or prevent all the wrongs in the world, but it must redress and prevent those "which are wrong to the nation itself." Mandated by the Constitution to provide for the general welfare, a strong national government must exercise a moral authority over the whole people, and serve as the nation's moral arbiter with virtually unlimited power to enforce its decisions. Wrongs must be prevented, he contended, by "either *congresses* or *courts*," reflecting (and filtering, if his past statements were a guide) the will of the people. Who, and by what standard, was to determine what was right and what was wrong, what promoted the general welfare and what did not? Lincoln offered no long-range formula, but in the short run there was no doubt that he regarded the Republican party as the party of moral rectitude. To Douglas, the differences between him and his challenger were unmistakable. Lincoln, he said, "goes for consolidation and uniformity in our government," while "I go for maintaining the confederation of the sovereign states." Consolidation or confederation. It was a question as old as the republic. [28]

Lincoln's irrepressible conflict, then, was a moral contest, to be fought until one side or the other achieved total victory. The restoration of the Missouri Compromise was no longer the solution to the slavery issue, as he had once argued, for that suggested the preservation of a half-slave, half-free Union and implied that there was some middle ground between right and wrong. The conflict now was directed toward higher goals—the total elimination of slavery from all the territories and the ultimate extinction of slavery in the Southern states. The real issue separating the North and the South, Lincoln ordained, was the "eternal struggle between . . . right and wrong—throughout the world." He saw himself in the role of a modern-day crusader, fighting for the "common right of humanity"

28. Notes for Speeches at Columbus and Cincinnati, Ohio, September 16, 17, 1859, in *Collected Works*, III, 435; Douglas at Springfield, July 17, 1858, in Paul M. Angle, ed., *Created Equal? The Complete Lincoln-Douglas Debates of 1858* (Chicago, 1958), 55.

in a contest that had been fought from the "beginning of time." He had found a place in history.

Lincoln's failure to win Douglas' senate seat was only a momentary setback. There was no retreat. "Another explosion will soon come," he predicted, but it would be an explosion without war or violence. Once the people recognized the "real difference" between the Republicans and their opposition, he was confident the controversy would be settled peaceably and correctly (an expression of faith after all in the sovereignty of the people, at least those in the free states where his party would have influence). It was a time for action. It was a time, he told party members following the 1858 decision, to hold conventions, adopt platforms, nominate candidates, and carry elections. For the right to prevail, he counseled, "we must employ instrumentalities." Politics had been invested with a moral purpose, but it was still politics nonetheless. In spite of Lincoln's distrust of popular sovereignty, he knew that the ultimate decision whether the United States would be all slave or all free would be a political decision. He was playing a dangerous game, as Douglas often reminded him, for the one element in the political process that was essential to a resolution of the slavery issue was almost totally missing from his game plan: the South.[29]

Douglas reproached Lincoln for his moral arrogance and his unwarranted insults against the Southern people. "It does not become Mr. Lincoln," he declared, to tell the people of the South that "they have no consciences, that they are living in a state of iniquity, and [that] they are cherishing an institution to their bosoms in violation of the law of God." The people of the slaveholding states, Douglas maintained, "are civilized men as well as ourselves, . . . they bear consciences as well as we, and . . . they are accountable to God and their posterity and not to us." But Lincoln seemed to care but little about the South, for the South offered no political threat to his cause. At the same time that he charged Southern leaders with seeking to nationalize slavery, he knew that they were powerless, by

29. Seventh and Last Debate with Stephen A. Douglas at Alton, Illinois, October 15, 1858, Lincoln to H. D. Sharpe, December 8, 1858, Lincoln to Henry Asbury, November 19, 1858, Speech at Cincinnati, Ohio, September 17, 1859, in *Collected Works*, III, 315–16, 344, 339, 460–61.

themselves, to achieve that goal. The extension of slavery into the states of the North could only "be reached by Douglas' route"; after 1858, Douglas' stock had so fallen in the South that there was little likelihood that he could ever be able to mobilize significant Southern support. Lincoln knew what many Republicans had begun to realize, that they could carry a national election without the support of a single Southern state.

Southerners' hostility toward the Republican party, Lincoln believed, was due only to their "ignorance and misapprehension" of the party's aims. Once Southerners understood Republican intentions and became convinced that since the party represented moral right it would be incapable of wronging the South, hostility would be dropped. Southerners, however, found it difficult to achieve that understanding. They were hardly reassured, for example, by Lincoln's promise not to disturb slavery in their states, at the same time that he announced the Republican party's "life-giving principle" to be "hatred to the institution of Slavery . . . in all its aspects, moral, social, and political." Nor were their minds set at ease when he invoked God's authority on behalf of the ultimate extinction of slavery and proclaimed an irrepressible conflict between right and wrong. They could hardly agree that the only way to avoid a national calamity was to place Lincoln at the helm of the republic. Lincoln's doctrines, observed one border-state editor, were the "most subtle and dangerous form of anti-slaveryism" because they were so ambiguous.[30]

In a rare acknowledgment of Southern concerns, in Cincinnati in the fall of 1859 when he addressed the Kentuckians across the Ohio River, Lincoln asked Southerners what they meant to do. Will you divide the Union whenever a Republican is elected president? "Will you make war upon us and kill us all?" As brave and gallant as Southerners were, they would be no match for the North. "Man for man," he warned, "you are not better than we are, and there are not

30. Sixth Debate with Stephen A. Douglas at Quincy, Illinois, October 13, 1858, Notes for Speeches at Columbus and Cincinnati, Ohio, September 16, 17, 1859, Speech at Beloit, Wisconsin, October 1, 1859, in *Collected Works*, III, 274–75 (Douglas' reply), 429, 482; Springfield *Illinois State Journal*, November 8, 1860; Louisville *Courier*, May 26, 1860, in Dwight L. Dumond, ed., *Southern Editorials on Secession* (New York, 1931), 115.

so many of you as there are of us. You will never make much of a hand at whipping us." Republicans, he declared, "intend to 'stand by our guns,' to be patient and firm, and in the long run to beat you." If there was to be violence, the responsibility would rest with the South.[31]

If Lincoln intended his warnings to reach Southern ears, he was probably disappointed, for few Southerners outside the border states (particularly Missouri and Kentucky) paid much attention to his statements. Some editors gave him passing notice in connection with the 1858 campaign, but, like a Mississippi paper, were indifferent whether he won or lost. The race between Douglas and Lincoln, it was said, was a "fight in which the South should feel no other concern than curiosity as to the result." Both were in the "service of freesoilism," both were "fighting under pirate colors." Others expressed a preference for Lincoln, on the ground that he could do nothing to harm the South, whereas Douglas could "do us harm to the extent of his influence and power."

Lincoln cared little whether the South noticed him or not. In the coming presidential contest, the South was clearly irrelevant (provided Douglas and the Southerners did not patch up their differences). The real battleground was in the North, and it was the Northern vote that would decide the election. In the meantime, Lincoln took seriously the many suggestions that he seek the Republican nomination for president. To his friend Lyman Trumbull, he confessed in characteristic understatement that "the taste *is* in my mouth a little." His invitations to speak outside Illinois multiplied. As he moved about the Northwest, addressing enthusiastic audiences, he cautioned Republicans to prepare for the contest carefully and deliberately, to soften their radicalism, to give highest priority to party unity, to avoid controversial statements ("say *nothing* on points where it is probable we shall disagree"), and, above all, to resist the temptation to dally with Douglas.[32]

31. Speech at Cincinnati, September 17, 1859, in *Collected Works*, III, 453–54.

32. Jackson *Mississippian*, September 14, 1858, quoted in Washington *Union*, September 22, 1858; Milledgeville (Ga.) *Federal Union*, September 14, 1858; Lincoln to Lyman Trumbull, April 29, 1860, Lincoln to Schuyler Colfax, July 6, 1859, Fragments: Notes for Speeches, ca. September, 1859, in *Collected Works*, IV, 45, III, 390–91, 398.

As Lincoln carefully calculated his next political moves, he became convinced that he was the only candidate who could unite the free states against Douglas. More and more Republicans, especially in the Western states, feared that if Seward were nominated, the Democrats and Douglas would surely win. Yet Seward remained the front-runner, casting a long shadow from which Lincoln did not fully emerge until the spring of 1860. It was testimony to Lincoln's political success, however, that he gradually assumed the role of one who would be acceptable to all elements in the party, radical enough to appeal to the abolitionists while espousing (when the occasion called for it) a conservative stance that satisfied the old-line Whigs. One Republican paper listed Lincoln's qualifications for the nation's highest office: A man of "unimpeachable purity . . . the most unspotted man of the Republic"; intellectual acuteness, "not learned in a bookish sense, but master of great fundamental principles"; and, most important, "right on the record." Lincoln was the "embodiment of the principles and measures necessary for the perpetuity of the Union and the preservation of our free institutions," was acceptable to "all shades of opinion, harmonizing all interests, conciliating all jarring elements," and was a "guarantor of success." The feeling grew among Republicans that Lincoln, if nominated and elected, would put an end to the sectional conflict, bring peace and harmony back to the country, and restore the ties of affection that once bound the North and South.[33]

Lincoln's confidence was shaken, suddenly and without warning, when news of John Brown's raid on Harpers Ferry burst onto the pages of the nation's press. To Southerners, the irrepressible conflict, preached by Lincoln and Seward, had unexpectedly arrived. The crisis has come, reported the Washington *Constitution*, the "danger is upon us." To a Memphis paper, it was the "beginning of the end." The raid, warned a New Orleans editor, was the first stage of the irrepressible conflict, the "beginning of a crusade against slavery all through the South" that would end only "with the utter extermination of the institution wherever it existed." To Douglas, the danger implicit in Lincoln's "house divided" doctrine, against which he had repeatedly warned, had been demonstrated. The raid, he

33. Chicago *Press and Tribune*, February 16, 1860.

declared, was the "natural, logical, inevitable result of the doctrines and teachings of the Republican party." [34]

Republicans were quick to denounce the "wild and lawless" move of a demented old man, lest the raid turn opinion against their party. Lincoln, never one to react without carefully weighing all the possible repercussions, waited until after Brown had been tried and sentenced before publicly responding. He left no doubt that he strongly disapproved of Brown's action. At the same time, he was careful not to anger the party's radical elements. While he praised Brown for his courage and his "rare unselfishness," he condemned the raid as a violation of the law, pointing out that it would have no effect on the ultimate extinction of slavery. Brown's belief that slavery was wrong did not justify "violence, bloodshed, and treason." His execution, Lincoln said, was right. He bristled at the effort to identify Brown with the Republican party, however, and turned the charge back on the attackers. It was not the teachings of the Republican party that provoked the raid, he stated, but rather the South's commitment to slavery. [35]

Nonetheless, Lincoln could hardly escape the sobering impact of the episode; nor can one assume that he was unmindful of the Southern fears that the crisis he had prophesied was underway. John Brown's raid was not the "new explosion" he had predicted. The raid, however, did stress the need for a less heated, less controversial approach to the coming presidential campaign. Lincoln's language became less harsh, less inflammatory, more conciliatory. He went to greater lengths to clear the Republican party of revolutionary or destructive intent. Talk of the ultimate extinction of slavery was muted. "We are not trying to destroy it," he emphasized. "The peace of society, and the structure of our government both require that we should let it alone, and we insist on letting it alone." While he privately maintained that the sentiments of his "House Divided"

34. Washington *Constitution*, December 17, 1859; Memphis *Avalanche*, quoted in Avery Craven, *The Growth of Southern Nationalism, 1848–1861* (Baton Rouge, 1953), 309; New Orleans *Daily Crescent*, December 20, 1860, in Dumond, ed., *Southern Editorials on Secession*, 355; Douglas, quoted in Johannsen, *Stephen A. Douglas*, 724.

35. Springfield *Illinois State Journal*, October 20, 21, 24, 1859; Speech at Elwood, Kansas, December 1 [November 30?], 1859, Speech at Leavenworth, Kansas, December 3, 1859, Second Speech at Leavenworth, Kansas, December 5, 1859, in *Collected Works*, III, 496, 502, 503.

speech still formed the basis of his position, he publicly charged his opponents with "bushwhackery" for their persistence in trying to pin the irrepressible conflict doctrine on the Republicans. After all, he observed, he and Seward had merely repeated what the "old fathers" had said many years before.[36]

If John Brown's raid was not the "new explosion" Lincoln expected, then was the 1860 election to be his irrepressible conflict? Or to put it another way: Was 1860 to be the crisis which Lincoln had said must be "reached and passed" before the slavery agitation would cease? Was 1860 to be the moment when, in the language of the "House Divided" speech, the "opponents of slavery will arrest the further spread of it and place it where the public mind shall rest in the belief that it is in the course of ultimate extinction"? Lincoln, in the fashion of a true politician, issued mixed signals, reassuring Southerners that he meant them no harm while emphasizing the need to settle the slavery question once and for all in the Republican way. The slavery issue can no more be avoided, he observed, "than a man can live without eating." The issue, he insisted, must be "taken up in earnest, and really settled." Only the election of a Republican to the presidency would end the "sectionalism and all the wrangling," for the Republican way was the "peaceful way, the old-fashioned way," the way of the nation's Founding Fathers. "We are the only true Union men."[37]

In his last important statement before his nomination, delivered at New York's Cooper Institute, Lincoln addressed the Southern people, "if they would listen," in an effort that can only be described as halfhearted. He felt compelled, at that late hour, to set their minds at ease by telling them what the Republican party was not—it was not sectional, not revolutionary, not responsible for the agitation over slavery. He did not say what the party was; presumably, the South would have to draw its own conclusions on that matter. Furthermore, he denied the legitimacy of Southern grievances against the North and, in a tone of defiance, dismissed the threats

36. Speech at Leavenworth, Kansas, December 3, 1859, Speech at Hartford, Connecticut, March 5, 1860, in *Collected Works*, III, 501, IV, 6.

37. Speech at New Haven, Connecticut, March 6, 1860, Speech at Mechanicsburg, Illinois, November 4, 1859, in *Collected Works*, IV, 15, 17, III, 493.

of some in the South to break up the Union rather than submit to a Republican president as simply a "rule or ruin" attitude.

In any case, it was not the South that mattered. All that stood in the way of "an early and complete success of Republicanism," Lincoln wrote Ohio's Salmon P. Chase, was "Douglasism." The choice was clear. It was either the Republican way, resting firmly on the "profound central truth that slavery is wrong and ought to be dealt with as a wrong," or it was the way of Douglas and the Slave Power. If the latter, the people in the free states must suppress all their feelings that slavery is wrong and must join with Southerners in calling it right; they must arrest and return the South's fugitive slaves "with greedy pleasure"; they must "pull down" the free state constitutions; and they must "throw open the Free Territories" to the expansion of slavery. It was an alarming scenario.

Contrary to what Lincoln had once argued, there was no middle ground, for in a contest between right and wrong there could be no compromise. In the past, he noted, "our best and greatest men" had consistently "underestimated the size" of the slavery question. Their efforts to settle it had proven temporary and evanescent, for they brought forth only "small cures for great sores—plasters too small to cover the wound." Republicans, he vowed, would make no such mistakes. Their position was right, unalterable, and "never for a moment to be lost sight of." [38]

The election of 1860, Lincoln seemed to be saying, was to be the final showdown between the "opposing and enduring" forces, a contest that would determine whether this would be a free or a slave nation. Either the Republicans would succeed, and slavery would be placed "in the course of ultimate extinction," or the Republicans would be defeated, and slavery would "become alike lawful in all the States, old as well as new—North as well as South." Although he carefully avoided the phrase, the irrepressible conflict was at hand.

---

38. Address at Cooper Institute, New York City, February 27, 1860, Lincoln to Salmon P. Chase, September 21, 1859, Speech at Manchester, New Hampshire, March 1, 1860, Speech at New Haven, Connecticut, March 6, 1860, in *Collected Works*, III, 535, 536–43, 471, 551, IV, 15.

4

Lincoln and the South in 1860

On November 8, 1860, two days after the presidential election had been decided, Stephen A. Douglas arrived in New Orleans, where he was greeted by a large group of well-wishers. It was his last public appearance on what had been a strenuous and fatiguing campaign tour through the states of the Deep South, confronting hostile audiences with his message that the election of a Republican president was not sufficient reason for secession. He had been convinced for some time that Lincoln would win. The election returns bore him out. Before he left New Orleans to continue his journey homeward, he responded to an appeal by the city's financial and business leadership for a statement on the condition of the country.

No man, Douglas said, regretted Abraham Lincoln's election more than he, and no one was more prepared to resist the policies which Lincoln represented. But, he emphasized, the mere election of any man to the presidency, in accordance with the Constitution and laws, did not "furnish any just cause or reasonable ground for dissolving the Federal Union." Lincoln, he argued, was more to be pitied than feared. The Democrats had captured the House of Representatives and continued to control the Senate; the Supreme Court, safe from Republican influence, would "restrain all illegal and unconstitutional acts" of the new administration. Thus "tied hand and foot," Lincoln would be "utterly powerless for evil," even if he should be disposed "to do wrong." "What good or harm can he do to anybody?" Douglas asked. Four years would soon pass away. Southerners must bide their time, until the ballot box would furnish a "peaceful, legal and constitutional remedy for all the evils and grievances with which the country may be afflicted." Douglas concluded with a moving tribute to the Union, and appealed to the patriotism of the Southern people, asking that they turn away from those who would destroy the republic.[1]

It is useless, although interesting, to speculate on how the course of history might have been changed had Douglas' advice been heeded. Had the South heeded Douglas' advice, Lincoln would be known today as simply one of many Northern politicians who tried to walk the thin line between the restriction of slavery on the one hand and the toleration of it on the other; in 1860 one politician suggested that as president, Lincoln would be as good as Buchanan and no worse than Fillmore.

But historians must deal with what did happen, not with what did not. The fact is, the South did not accept Douglas' advice. Indeed, following his stand against slavery in the proposed state of Kansas and his alternative interpretation of the Dred Scott decision, Southerners had ceased accepting him. They had reacted angrily to his strong Union statements during the campaign, and especially to what they called his "hateful edict" ("Black Republican slang on Southern soil," according to one source) that the new president, whoever he might be, should handle the secessionists as firmly as Jackson had handled South Carolina's nullifiers in 1832. Indeed, to many in the South, Douglas had exceeded even the Republicans in the strident tone of his rhetoric. "Even Lincoln, the Rail Mauler," wrote a Georgia editor, had a "better idea of decency and dignity" than did Douglas, for Lincoln had made no such statements. In fact, Lincoln had made no statements at all.[2]

1. Robert W. Johannsen, *Stephen A. Douglas* (New York, 1973), 805–807; Douglas to Ninety-Six New Orleans Citizens, November 13, 1860, in Johannsen, ed., *The Letters of Stephen A. Douglas* (Urbana, 1961), 499–503. Similar views were suggested in some Southern papers; for example, see the New Orleans *Picayune*, October 24, November 8, 15, 1860; and the Richmond *Enquirer*, November 9, 1860.

2. Alexander H. Stephens to J. Henly Smith, July 10, 1860, in U. B. Phillips, ed., *The Correspondence of Robert Toombs, Alexander H. Stephens, and Howell Cobb* (Washington, D.C., 1913), 487; Charleston *Mercury*, August 30, September 3, 1860; Milledgeville (Ga.) *Federal Union*, September 25, October 2, 1860. Some Southern papers

The day after Douglas' statement appeared in the press, a writer in the New Orleans *Crescent* remarked that "we never read anything from the pen of Senator Douglas which gave us so little satisfaction. It would have been better had he not said a word." If Southerners spurned Douglas' advice to cool their emotions, what then were they afraid of? Lincoln and the Republicans were puzzled, for they saw no reason for the South's unhappiness. Lincoln had claimed on a number of occasions that his election would end the agitation over slavery. He believed that once Southerners recognized that he was right, they would cease their hostility toward the North. James Russell Lowell was certain that Lincoln's election would end the sectional excitement, for it would be apparent that the Republican party was founded on an "enduring principle." William H. Seward, the most prominent Republican spokesman, predicted there would be "no dangers, disasters, or calamities" as a result of Lincoln's election. Even the militant abolitionist William Lloyd Garrison agreed that Lincoln would "do nothing to offend the South." Following Lincoln's election, Horace Greeley was convinced that everything in the country would be back to normal in a very short time.[3]

Some Southern voices picked up the Republican refrain, pointing out that Lincoln was clearly with the "conservative element" of his party and that he posed no threat to Southern institutions. An anonymous cotton planter suggested that Lincoln would even protect slavery and the sovereignty of the Southern states, for he would "walk in the footsteps of Henry Clay and President Fillmore." "Would not that satisfy every Constitutional Union-loving Southern

---

saw little difference between Douglas and Lincoln, and predicted that Douglas would be Lincoln's "right-hand man" in coercing the South to comply with Republican doctrines; Charleston *Mercury*, September 24, 1860; Montgomery *Daily Mail*, July 6, 1860, quoted in Avery O. Craven, *The Growth of Southern Nationalism, 1848–1861* (Baton Rouge, 1953), 342.

3. New Orleans *Daily Crescent*, November 15, 1860, in Dwight L. Dumond, ed., *Southern Editorials on Secession* (New York, 1931), 241; "The Election in November," *Atlantic Monthly*, VI (October, 1860), 502; Seward, Speech at Detroit, September 4, 1860, in George E. Baker, ed., *The Works of William H. Seward* (5 vols.; New York and Boston, 1853–84), IV, 316; Garrison to Oliver Johnson, August 9, 1860, in Louis Ruchames, ed., *From Disunionism to the Brink of War* (Cambridge, Mass., 1975), 687, Vol. IV of *The Letters of William Lloyd Garrison*, 6 vols.; New York *Tribune*, October 31, 1860.

man?" he asked. Most Southerners, however, looked with deep suspicion upon the efforts to soothe their fears. After having been maligned during the campaign, one Southern editor complained, they were now told "that Mr. Lincoln is a very good man, a very amiable man; . . . not at all violent in his prejudices or partialities; that, on the contrary, he is a moderate, kindly-tempered, conservative man." Southerners were told that if they would only submit to Lincoln's administration, they would quickly realize "that he will make one of the best Presidents the South or the country ever had!" To a New Orleans editor, there was only one way to interpret the Republican assurances: "Will you walk into my parlor said the spider to the fly." Wary of Northern motives, suspicious of Northern intentions, people in the South were advised to look to Lincoln himself. "We propose to measure Mr. Lincoln by his own standard."[4]

But what was that standard? Lincoln was not well enough known in the South for Southerners to answer that question with any degree of certainty. Lincoln's political career, the Chicago *Tribune* had pointed out, had been "confined to a very limited sphere."[5] His political campaigns as an antislavery activist were seldom reported outside his state, and even within Illinois his statements often seemed but echoes of speeches already made by better-known figures like Seward, Salmon P. Chase, and Charles Sumner. It was not until 1858, when Lincoln challenged Douglas for a seat in the United States Senate, that his name became known outside Illinois, but even then it was hardly the "house-hold word" claimed by his supporters. In the South, he was scarcely mentioned, and then only in passing as the man who had assumed the unenviable role of a "Giant Killer," an obscure, inexperienced frontier lawyer who sought to advance his political career by debating the nationally known and controversial Senator Douglas.

The South's first surprise came when the Republicans nominated that obscure frontier lawyer for the presidency. Seward was thought

4. Charlottesville (Va.) *Review*, November 23, 1860, in Dumond, ed., *Southern Editorials on Secession*, 263; Washington *National Intelligencer*, November 13, 1860; Richmond *Enquirer*, October 5, 1860; New Orleans *Daily Crescent*, November 12, 1860, in Dumond, ed., *Southern Editorials on Secession*, 229; Charleston *Courier*, November 5, 1860.

5. Chicago *Press and Tribune*, October 29, 1858.

to have the nomination in the bag, but if not Seward, then such men as Chase, Frémont, or Edward Bates were thought to be next in line. Lincoln was not among those mentioned. As they puzzled over the unexpected turn of events at the Chicago convention, Southerners suspected something sinister and conspiratorial. The Charleston *Mercury* concluded that Seward had been cast aside because he would have been more disposed to "temporize with the South." Lincoln, on the other hand, was a "relentless, dogged, free-soil border-ruffian, . . . a vulgar mobocrat and a Southern hater in political opinions." When they nominated Lincoln, the Republicans ignored "all the intellect and decency of their party."[6]

As they groped for explanations of why Lincoln had been nominated and not Seward, Southern editors became convinced that Lincoln was the more dangerous of the two. His "House Divided" speech was recalled—a speech in which Lincoln not only declared that the contest between the North and South over slavery was an irrepressible conflict, incapable of compromise, but also predicted that the agitation would continue until slavery was either abolished everywhere or everywhere extended. Lincoln was the real author of the irrepressible conflict doctrine; Seward, it appeared, had only borrowed it from Lincoln. The Richmond *Enquirer* argued that Lincoln's nomination revealed the "determined hostility" of Republicans toward slavery, for unlike Seward, Lincoln was an "illiterate partisan . . . possessed only of his inveterate hatred of slavery." He had been nominated because he surpassed Seward in the "bitterness of his prejudice and the insanity of his fanaticism." Lincoln was the more dangerous of the two, observed the New York *Herald*, because he held all of Seward's "revolutionary and destructive theories" without the safeguard of Seward's "practical and experienced statesmanship." Even Lincoln's law partner and confidant, William H. Herndon, later recalled that it was Lincoln's "House Divided" speech that "drove the nail into Seward's political coffin."[7]

6. Donald E. Reynolds, *Editors Make War: Southern Newspapers in the Secession Crisis* (Nashville, 1970), 54–58; Charleston *Mercury*, October 15, 1860; Charleston *Courier*, May 24, 1860.

7. Richmond *Enquirer*, May 21, 1860; New York *Herald*, May 19, 20, 1860; William H. Herndon and Jesse W. Weik, *Herndon's Life of Lincoln*, ed. Paul M. Angle (Cleveland, 1949), 326–27.

Lincoln's nomination, Southerners feared, could only be explained as a conspiracy against their way of life. He would be but a figurehead, a tool of the abler, more powerful leaders in the Republican party. "An individual so obscure as he is," commented a South Carolinian, "could hardly be chosen President, unless as an agent of some strong and intelligent organization." It was no accident that Republicans had turned to Lincoln. The fact that he was "so little of anybody" was precisely the reason he was selected, for the Republicans seemed determined to carry on a campaign of "cant and humbug, based upon the fact that the American people know nothing of the candidate."[8]

As the 1860 campaign got under way, the signals coming out of the North were disturbingly mixed. Lincoln, said some of his supporters, was a "radical up to the limit to which the party . . . proposes to go," but, they also said, he was by nature a conservative who carefully avoided extremes. Others pointed out that Lincoln combined a radicalism on the slavery question with a constitutional conservatism that was manifested in a respect for existing institutions and laws. He was, it appeared, a man upon whom both radicals and conservatives could unite, one who was acceptable to "all shades of opinion." Clearly, such statements were meant to satisfy the diversity of opinion among Republicans; they only confused Southerners.[9]

Republican leaders, moreover, identified Lincoln with their own views, frequently putting words into Lincoln's mouth. Not long after the nomination, Charles Sumner mounted a vicious attack in the Senate against what he called the "barbarism of slavery." Slavery, he charged, was a barbarous institution, and Southerners who embraced it were barbarians with no claim to civilization. Many Republicans were shocked, yet the speech was reprinted and distributed by their congressional campaign committee. Sumner sent a copy to Lincoln, with a letter in which he expressed the hope that his remarks would unite Republicans and inspire "good men every-

8. Charleston *Courier*, October 20, 1860; Charleston *Mercury*, July 20, May 23, 1860. *Harper's Weekly* (June 2, 1860, p. 338) attributed Lincoln's nomination to the machinations of Horace Greeley, the creator and "censor" of the Republican party and the editor of "its great central organ."

9. Chicago *Press and Tribune*, May 15, February 16, 26, 1860.

where to join in their support." Lincoln, obviously disturbed, responded with a brief, noncommittal note. Speaking later in New York, Sumner predicted that with Lincoln's election, slavery would die "as a poisoned rat dies of rage in its hole." Comments like these received considerable attention in the Southern press, and it does not require much imagination to appreciate their impact on Southern opinion. One editor was grateful that Sumner had stripped away all the pretense and hypocrisy of the Republican party, thus exposing its true colors.[10]

Few Republican statements received so much attention in the Southern press as Seward's campaign address in Boston in August, probably because Southerners viewed Seward as reflecting Lincoln's position more accurately than any other Republican. Seward told his New England audience that the party had selected a candidate who "confesses the obligation of that higher law" which John Quincy Adams had proclaimed, and who "avows himself a soldier on the side of freedom in the irrepressible conflict between freedom and slavery." Like Sumner, Seward assured his listeners that Lincoln's election would end slavery in the United States. John Quincy Adams, higher law, irrepressible conflict, an end to slavery—coming at the South all at once, it is little wonder that Southerners feared the worst if Lincoln should be elected. To one Southerner, only God could preserve the nation from the evils of such "lying prophets."[11]

Less disturbing, perhaps, but nonetheless bothersome were the descriptions of the campaign Lincoln's party was waging in the North. The raucous, wild, and jovial exhibitions seemed to confirm

10. Charles Sumner, *The Barbarism of Slavery. Speech . . . on the Bill for the Admission of Kansas as a State, June 4, 1860* (Washington, D.C., 1860), 3; New York *Herald*, June 5, 6, 7, 1860; David Donald, *Charles Sumner and the Coming of the Civil War* (New York, 1960), 358, 360–61; Washington *Constitution*, July 28, 1860; Sumner to Lincoln, June 6, 1860, in Abraham Lincoln Papers, Library of Congress; Lincoln to Sumner, June 14, 1860, in *The Collected Works of Abraham Lincoln*, ed. Roy P. Basler et al. (9 vols.; New Brunswick, N.J., 1953), IV, 76; New York *Tribune*, July 12, 1860; New Orleans *Bee*, June 25, 1860, in Dumond, ed., *Southern Editorials on Secession*, 133.

11. Baker, ed., *Works of Seward*, IV, 83; Charleston *Mercury*, August 20, 1860; Louisville *Daily Journal*, August 22, 1860, in Dumond, ed., *Southern Editorials on Secession*, 164–65; Milledgeville (Ga.) *Federal Union*, October 2, 1860; Richmond *Enquirer*, August 27, 1860.

the *Herald*'s description of Lincoln as a "rough-spun disputatious village politician." The campaign, marked by barbecues and rallies, parades and flags, and banners and transparencies bearing slogans and catchwords, was reminiscent of that earlier presidential race when serious issues were overshadowed by log cabins and hard-cider jugs. The image of William Henry Harrison as the simple, God-fearing man of nature found a counterpart in the person of Abraham Lincoln. When two delegates to the Illinois Republican convention entered the hall carrying fence rails they said had been split by Lincoln, a new election symbol was born. Lincoln became the "Rail Candidate for President," and headlines in Republican papers screamed "Honest Old Abe. The People's Candidate for President. Rails and Flat-Boats. Log Cabins and Hard Cider Come Again." One paper boasted, in large, bold capitals, that Lincoln had "SPLIT THREE THOUSAND RAILS" in 1830 alone.[12]

Southerners were not impressed. Instead, they felt that the Republicans were deliberately trying to keep the issues from the electorate. "The Republicans say that Abraham Lincoln was once a rail-splitter and flatboatman," commented a Memphis paper. "Such low-flung catch-words as these are to be relied upon to seduce the Northern people into Abraham's bosom." Other papers noted that songbooks containing the "vilest doggerel" in praise of Lincoln were being distributed, brass medals bearing his likeness were being struck, and old rails (probably imported from New Jersey, scoffed one Southerner) were being put on display throughout the North. Rail Splitters' Battalions and Flatboat Associations sprang into existence. Floats featuring men splitting rails were dragged through the streets of towns and villages, alongside flatboats on wheels manned by Republicans in "romantic boatman's dress" plying oars in imaginary water. The campaign, noted the Charleston *Mercury*, had assumed an "intensely disgusting phase."

All the hoopla disturbed Southerners the more as they tried to gain some inkling of who Lincoln was, what he believed, and what

12. New York *Herald*, May 23, 1860; Chicago *Press and Tribune*, May 19, 1860; H. Preston James, "Political Pageantry in the Campaign of 1860 in Illinois," *Abraham Lincoln Quarterly*, IV (September, 1947), 313–47.

he would do if elected president. "It is humiliating," remarked one leader, "to see a party in this country putting forward a man for the Presidential chair, once occupied by Washington and Jefferson, whose only achievements have been that he split a few hundred rails in early life." Southerners realized what they had suspected all along, that the presidential campaign would be fought primarily in the North, that whoever carried the free states of the North would win the election, that they were little more than bystanders in what purported to be a national referendum. Either the Republicans, they thought, were unaware of the critical importance of the election and failed to take seriously the signs of impending disunion, or they were deliberately obscuring the issues in order to gain political advantage. The summer of 1860, they predicted, was likely to be "one of the greatest political excitements ever known in the history of this country," for its results would determine "the *destinies of the Republic.*" Republican indifference in the face of these signs seemed inexplicable. One Georgia editor concluded that the Republicans' choice of symbol was perhaps fitting after all. The maul, he wrote, was an instrument for splitting rails; Lincoln was to be the instrument for splitting the Union.[13]

No presidential candidate of a major party had been so little known at the time of his nomination, or had so little administrative and legislative experience as Lincoln. Untried in "public station," observed the pro-Southern Washington *Constitution*, Lincoln was "utterly unknown in the higher annals of American politics," lacking in the knowledge, experience, and statesmanship required of one who aspires to the highest office in the land. The Republican convention, it was said, could hardly have selected an individual with fewer "claims upon the confidence of the country."

The press, caught off guard, searched frantically for biographical details, while would-be biographers and printmakers scrambled to meet the demand for information on the nominee. In a dispatch filed at the conclusion of the Chicago convention, the New York *Times*

13. Memphis *Bulletin*, quoted in Charleston *Mercury*, May 30, 1860; Charleston *Mercury*, May 31, July 20, August 8, 1860; *De Bow's Review*, XXVIII (June, 1860), 742; Milledgeville (Ga.) *Federal Union*, September 4, 1860.

correspondent noted that "great inquiry" was being made into Lincoln's history. "The only evidence that he has a history as yet discovered," wrote the reporter, "is that he had a stump canvass with Mr. Douglas, in which he was beaten." Two books had recently been published to aid Americans in evaluating their candidates, each containing biographical sketches of those who had been "prominently suggested" for the presidency, but neither included the name of Abraham Lincoln (although one offered biographies of thirty-four men). A Southern magazine editor, J. D. B. De Bow, concluded that Lincoln's claims to the presidency had been considered "too contemptible" for him to be included. The only source conveniently at hand in many editorial offices was Charles Lanman's outdated *Dictionary of the United States Congress*, which summarized Lincoln's career up to the time he was elected to the House of Representatives in 1846 in one brief sentence.[14]

"Old Abe Lincoln is the hue and cry among all Black Republicans," commented a Charleston paper. "Enterprising booksellers are puzzling their brains to find ingenious litterateurs, with prolific imaginations, to manufacture lives of Abram Lincoln." It was clear to one Southern editor that Lincoln had never done anything to raise himself "above the sphere of a rollicking cross road politician"; others complained that even the Republicans had thought so little of Lincoln that they had failed to distribute a "memoir" of his life to newspaper offices. What they did not know was that the staff of the Chicago *Press and Tribune*, anticipating the "ten thousand inquiries" that would follow Lincoln's nomination, had prepared a biographical article that was sent to Republican editors throughout the North. It was apparently not part of the Republican strategy to supply information to Southerners (or even to the Northern Democratic press, for that matter). As a consequence, the first efforts to relate

14. Washington *Constitution*, May 19, 1860; New York *Times*, May 19, 1860; John Savage, *Our Living Representative Men* (Philadelphia, 1860), iii; D. W. Bartlett, *Presidential Candidates: Containing Sketches, Biographical, Personal and Political, of Prominent Candidates for the Presidency in 1860* (New York, 1859); De Bow's *Review*, XXIX (July, 1860), 100–101; Charles Lanman, *Dictionary of the United States Congress, Containing Biographical Sketches of Its Members from the Foundation of the Government* (Philadelphia, 1859), 298; Charleston *Courier*, May 19, 1860. Lanman sent Lincoln a copy of his *Dictionary* shortly after his nomination. See *Collected Works*, IV, 74.

the details of Lincoln's life in many parts of the country were fragmentary, incomplete, and often wrong.[15]

Lincoln himself supplied biographical details on two occasions: first, late in 1859 he gave information to his friend Jesse Fell, which was expanded and printed in a little-known Pennsylvania paper; and second, following his nomination, he supplied details to John Locke Scripps, an editor of the Chicago *Tribune*, which formed the basis for one of Lincoln's more popular campaign biographies. Anticipating the direction of his campaign, he placed heavy emphasis on the events of his early life, to the exclusion of meaningful information on his recent career as an antislavery politician. Perhaps it was a deliberate omission, for it was his humble, frontier origins and his pioneer character that would capture the popular imagination, not his role in the sectional polarization over the slavery issue. When he ended his statement to Fell with the 1854 passage by Congress of the Kansas-Nebraska Act, at the very threshold of the most important period in his career, Lincoln wrote that "what I have done since then, is pretty well known"—which, of course, was not true.

Following his nomination, however, the demands for biographical information became so heavy that Lincoln refused all further requests, on the ground that it was "impossible for him to attend to them." Indeed, he became increasingly sensitive on the matter, moved to anger on one occasion when a campaign biography was advertised as having been authorized by him. He was determined, he wrote, not to authorize anything that his adversaries could use "to make points upon without end." Controversy was to be avoided at all costs. One campaign publication, by the Illinois abolitionist Ichabod Codding, was allegedly suppressed by Republican leaders not only because it suggested that Lincoln was sympathetic toward the abolition of slavery but also because it noted several objections that had been made against him, including the charge that he favored the political equality of blacks. Another campaign biography was severely censored ("literally emasculated") as a result of pres-

---

15. Charleston *Courier*, May 31, June 2, 1860; Shepherdstown (Va.) *Register*, and New Orleans *Picayune*, quoted in Reynolds, *Editors Make War*, 54, 55; Chicago *Press and Tribune*, May 19, 1860; Ernest James Wessen, "Campaign Lives of Abraham Lincoln, 1860," in *Papers in Illinois History, 1937* (Springfield, 1938), 191.

sure from the party, because it included passages deemed dangerous to Lincoln's candidacy.[16]

A cursory examination of available campaign biographies suggests that they were directed toward Northern voters, not surprising since the Republicans neither needed nor expected Southern support. The principal threat to the party's success came not from the South but from Douglas and his followers in the North, and Republican leaders still feared that the Little Giant might draw votes away from their ticket. The campaign biographers generally portrayed Lincoln as a national conservative, in sharp contrast with Douglas, whom they charged with seeking the extension of slavery throughout the country. William Dean Howells' biography, which had some circulation in the South, deliberately omitted the "House Divided" speech, as well as all other speeches made in the 1858 campaign against Douglas. Others promised an end to the crisis over slavery if Lincoln should be elected. Lincoln was repeatedly pictured as America's "representative man." Elihu Washburne, an Illinois congressman and friend of Lincoln, declared that Lincoln wished only to serve his country. "One of the people, taken up by the people, he will be President of the people." But which people? Clearly, there was little in Lincoln with which Southerners could identify. Even the conservative New Orleans *Picayune* found little comfort in Lincoln's image and background, warning its readers that the Republican nomination was a hostile move toward the South and that Lincoln's election would endanger the Union.[17]

If Lincoln's campaign biographies fell short of calming Southern

16. Lincoln to Fell, December 20, 1859, Autobiography for John L. Scripps, June, 1860, Lincoln to Applicants for Biographical Data, June, 1860, Lincoln to Samuel Galloway, June 19, 1860, in *Collected Works*, III, 511–12, IV, 60–67, 79–80; Wessen, "Campaign Lives," 197–98, 196; "Codding's 'Republican Manual for the Campaign—1860,'" *Lincoln Lore*, No. 1490 (April, 1962), 2. Fell's statement, expanded from other sources, appeared in the *Chester County Times*, February 11, 1860, reprinted in Herbert Mitgang, ed., *Lincoln as They Saw Him* (New York, 1956), 146–52; for Scripps's biography, see Roy P. Basler and Lloyd A. Dunlap, eds., *Life of Abraham Lincoln* (New York, 1968).

17. William Dean Howells, *Lives and Speeches of Abraham Lincoln and Hannibal Hamlin* (Columbus, Ohio, 1860); Elihu B. Washburne, *Abraham Lincoln, His Personal History and Public Record. Speech of Hon. E. B. Washburne, of Illinois. Delivered in the U.S. House of Representatives, May 29, 1860* (Washington, D.C., 1860), 7; New Orleans *Picayune*, May 20, 1860.

fears, so also did Lincoln's pictures—or so it seems from some of the comments in the Southern press. Like people throughout the country, Southerners were curious as to what he looked like. Print-makers and engravers, no less than the journalists and biographers, rushed to meet the demand for pictures of Lincoln. Already expect-ing the worst of the Republican nominee, Southerners found little comfort in his appearance. When *Harper's Weekly* printed a woodcut based on a Mathew Brady photograph taken early in 1860 (see fron-tispiece), the Charleston *Mercury* saw only a "horrid-looking wretch . . . sooty and scoundrelly in aspect; a cross between the nutmeg dealer, the horse-swapper, and the nightman." Others echoed the *Mercury*'s assessment. Lincoln's portrait, commented another paper, was "enough to scare one out of a night's rest." Much was made of an episode reportedly occurring at Saratoga Springs when some wag passed off a portrait of Lincoln as being that of the notorious pirate Jean Lafitte. Before the joke was revealed, one unsuspecting Repub-lican agreed that Lincoln's visage exhibited piratical qualities.[18]

Lincoln was nominated for the presidency on May 16; the nation's voters would not cast their ballots until November 6. By midsum-mer, Lincoln was telling his friends that he would be elected, that the success of the Republican ticket was inevitable. Southerners soon reached the same conclusion. "As sure as night follows the setting sun," declared the Richmond *Enquirer* in August, "Lincoln, the one-idea, Black Republican Abolitionist, will be the next Presi-dent of the United States." When the Republicans swept the Octo-ber state elections in the North, Lincoln's success became a cer-tainty—and Douglas left for the Deep South to campaign against secession.

For six and a half months, from nomination to election, Lincoln remained at home in Springfield, receiving visitors and answering correspondence, while the rest of the country speculated on what he would do once he was elected. The speculation did not subside fol-lowing his election, but increased as several of the slave states began moving toward secession. Lincoln felt a little more free to leave his

18. *Harper's Weekly*, May 26, 1860, p. 320; Charleston *Mercury*, June 7, July 3, 1860; Charleston *Courier*, July 6, 1860. For an excellent study of the prints of Lincoln issued during the campaign, see Harold Holzer, Gabor S. Boritt, and Mark E. Neely, Jr., *The Lincoln Image: Abraham Lincoln and the Popular Print* (New York, 1984).

home following his election, relieved, he said, that he was no longer "shut up in Springfield," but he still kept his public exposure at a bare minimum.[19]

Lincoln did not lack for advice on how to respond to the speculation. Friends, political colleagues, newspaper editors and correspondents, well-wishers of all sorts were unhesitating in their suggestions on how he should behave during the campaign. He also kept in close touch with the Republican National Committee in New York, seeking counsel on how he should react to the requests for public statements and invitations to public gatherings. The advice he received from the national party was clear and unequivocal: he was to remain silent on the issues of the election; he was to make no statements, write no public letters, refrain from traveling, and authorize no one to speak or write for him.

Maintain a "masterly silence," wrote a member of the national committee, and after the election maintain an "equally 'masterly inactivity.'" "Maintain the grand effect of your eloquent silence," advised another supporter. Whether or not Lincoln's silence was masterly or eloquent, it was also, in the judgment of recent historians, a perilous silence. For Lincoln to speak out on the issues, however, was to risk the election. He knew only too well that the Republican party was a fragile coalition of radical antislavery enthusiasts and constitutional conservatives, a party that was guided, as one Southern writer put it, by "two distinct sets of spirits." Any statement that would relieve Southern tensions, he was told, would disgust "thousands of the best and finest Republicans in the country." It was more important to retain a strong and united support within the party than to worry about Southern threats. Besides, Lincoln was informed by the national committee, there was no "real danger" of the secession of a single slave state. Even if there were, there would be time enough for Lincoln to react after he assumed the duties of the presidential office.[20]

From the moment of his nomination, the strategy of silence was

19. Lincoln to Anson G. Henry, July 4, 1860, Lincoln to Simeon Francis, August 4, 1860, Remarks at Lincoln, Illinois, November 21, 1860, in *Collected Works*, IV, 82, 90, 143; Richmond *Enquirer*, August 17, 1860.

20. George Fogg to Lincoln, October 26, 1860, William Hunt to Lincoln, December 13, 1860, in Lincoln Papers, Library of Congress; Avery Craven, "Southern At-

urged on Lincoln from virtually every quarter. William Cullen Bryant, whose New York newspaper supported the Republican ticket, cautioned Lincoln that he would save himself and his party a lot of trouble by refraining from writing letters or making speeches. "Do nothing at present," Bryant advised, "but allow yourself to be elected." From the abolitionist Joshua R. Giddings, with whom Lincoln had served in Congress many years before, came the suggestion that he follow the example of John Quincy Adams rather than that of Henry Clay. Adams, Giddings reminded Lincoln, had refused to express an opinion even to his most intimate friends. Clay, on the other hand, went down to defeat because he tried "to make his opinions acceptable to all." Others, no doubt aware of the esteem in which Lincoln held Clay, echoed the advice. "Write *nothing for publication*," demanded a Pennsylvania Republican. "The 'cacoether scribendi' [that is, the irresistible urge to write] killed Mr. Clay. For God's sake . . . do not let it kill you!"[21]

Lincoln had no problem following the advice, for to maintain a consistent silence was as much his own inclination as it was the party's directive. Sitting in the calm, friendly atmosphere of his hometown, surrounded by friends and admirers, Lincoln was insulated from the crisis that threatened the Union. Indeed, the crisis appeared much less serious on the prairies of central Illinois than it did in the legislative halls and executive offices of the national capi-

---

titudes Toward Lincoln," *Papers in Illinois History, 1942* (Springfield, 1943), 7; David M. Potter, *Lincoln and His Party in the Secession Crisis* (New Haven, 1962), 20, 23; New Orleans *Bee*, June 25, 1860, in Dumond, ed., *Southern Editorials on Secession*, 131. Fogg (a member of the national committee), in cautioning Lincoln not to travel, noted that the "trials of Douglas in search of his 'father's grave,' and his 'anxious mother's' *pantry*, are freely commented on by the Republican papers who hold up your quiet and dignified retirement in contrast." If Lincoln should travel, it would "relieve Douglas of the charge of being the only stump candidate for the Presidency." Fogg to Lincoln, August 18, 1860, in Lincoln Papers, Library of Congress.

21. William Cullen Bryant to Lincoln, June 16, 1860, Joshua R. Giddings to Lincoln, June 19, 1860, John Fry to Lincoln, August 9, 1860, in Lincoln Papers, Library of Congress. For a study of Lincoln's silence during the period following his election, see Robert G. Gunderson, "Lincoln and the Policy of Eloquent Silence: November, 1860, to March, 1861," *Quarterly Journal of Speech*, XLVII (February, 1961), 1–9; and Waldo W. Braden, " 'Kindly Let Me Be Silent': A Reluctant Lincoln," *Lincoln Herald*, LXXXVI (Winter, 1984), 195–202, reprinted in Waldo W. Braden, *Abraham Lincoln, Public Speaker* (Baton Rouge, 1988), 37–47.

tal, which may explain why Douglas was so alarmed that he threw precedent to the winds and took his appeal for the Union into the heart of the slaveholding South. Lincoln shared what Allan Nevins has called the "cardinal error of the Republicans" in the 1860 election: a failure to regard the danger of secession "with the candor and emphasis which it required." In earlier years, he had treated what he called the "bugbear of disunion" with scorn and ridicule, and he saw little reason to alter his attitude in 1860. "The people of the South," he confidently proclaimed, "have too much of good sense, and good temper to attempt the ruin of the government." One distraught visitor to Springfield reported that Lincoln "did not believe, could not be made to believe, that the South meant secession and war." When warned that Southerners were in "dead earnest," Lincoln only laughed. Even South Carolina's secession did not alter Lincoln's outlook. Although he conceded, in remarkable understatement, that the "political horizon looks dark and lowering," he was certain that the people would soon "set all right." [22]

To all who appealed to him for a statement that might ease the crisis, Lincoln responded with a form letter informing his correspondents that he had been advised "to write nothing whatever upon any point of political doctrine," on the ground that his positions on the issues were well known. To some, he felt a more personal explanation was in order. "By the lessons of the past [a reference to Clay's letter writing], and the united voice of all discreet friends," Lincoln wrote, "I am neither [to] write or speak a word for the public." And when he corresponded with his closest friends, he urged that his letters be burned because, he said, "it is best not to be known that I write at all." Lincoln adhered to this course of inaction throughout the campaign, and as the election neared, he proudly informed the national committee that there need be no concern that he would "precipitate a letter upon the public." Indeed, his silence became a virtue. "I am rather inclined to silence," he later remarked, "and whether that be wise or not, it is at least more unusual now-a-

---

22. Allan Nevins, *The Emergence of Lincoln* (2 vols.; New York, 1950), II, 305; Speech at Chicago, July 19, 1856, Lincoln to John B. Fry, August 15, 1860, Lincoln to Peter H. Silvester, December 22, 1860, in *Collected Works*, II, 349, IV, 95, 160; Charles M. Segal, ed., *Conversations with Lincoln* (New York, 1961), 45–46.

days to find a man who can hold his tongue than to find one who cannot."[23]

Southern editors were bemused by the cool nonchalance with which Republicans addressed the crisis. Statements like that of Horace Greeley's New York *Tribune*, that the South "could no more unite upon a scheme of secession, than a company of lunatics could conspire to break out of Bedlam," seemed more like a challenge than an expression of confidence. When a Philadelphia paper predicted that there would be no secession and that Lincoln's administration would be a "prosperous and peaceful one," a Charleston editor replied, "We Shall See." In spite of all the most convincing signs, commented the New Orleans *Bee*, "the people of the North appear afflicted with transcendental dubiety in respect to the earnestness and reality of Southern movements," a striking revelation of the "ignorance which pervades the North touching Southern sentiment."[24]

By election time, some members of Lincoln's party were getting nervous and began to question his silence. Rumors that a stock market panic would follow Lincoln's election moved Northern business and financial interests to ask for a public letter that would ease people's minds and disarm the mischief-makers. The New York *Times* observed that the crisis was attributable solely to Southern misunderstanding of the Republican party; a statement from Lincoln would correct the misunderstanding and end the crisis. Unionists in the border slave states begged Lincoln to issue an authoritative statement of his conservative views on the slavery question, in the hope that it would strengthen their opposition to the secession movement. "There is an epidemic insanity raging all over this country," wrote a Republican senator from Ohio, and a growing feeling that only Lincoln could calm it down.[25]

23. Form Reply to Requests for Political Opinions (signed by J. G. Nicolay), Lincoln to Samuel Galloway, June 19, 1860, Lincoln to Leonard Swett, May 30, 1860, Lincoln to Fogg, October 31, 1860, Remarks at the Monongahela House, Pittsburgh, Pennsylvania, February 14, 1861, in *Collected Works*, IV, 60, 80, 57, 135, 209.

24. New York *Tribune*, quoted in Charleston *Mercury*, August 3, 1860; Philadelphia *Bulletin*, quoted in Charleston *Courier*, October 13, 1860; New Orleans *Bee*, November 28, 1860, in Dumond, ed., *Southern Editorials on Secession*, 274.

25. George T. M. Davis to Jesse K. Dubois, October 20, 1860, Davis to Lincoln, October 31, 1860, Truman Smith to Lincoln, November 7, 1860, Henry J. Raymond to Lincoln, November 14, 1860, Thomas Corwin to Lincoln, November 4 (enclosing letter of S. W. Spencer, October 29), 1860, December 11, 1860, December 24, 1860,

Still Lincoln remained steadfast. "What is it I could say which would quiet alarm?" he asked. Simply to repeat what he had said many times before would give an impression of weakness and cowardice. He responded angrily to one visitor who suggested that a conservative statement would reassure those men who were "honestly alarmed." There were no such men, Lincoln shot back. It was all a trick, "the same old trick by which the South breaks down every Northern victory." If he should comply, he would lose the support of those who had nominated him. His first duty, he exclaimed, was to his party. Anyway, Southerners would not listen to him, and even if they did, they would not believe him.[26]

Lincoln had one stock response to those who pleaded with him for a statement: *Read my speeches.* From the moment of his nomination, he had advised those who wished to know where he stood to examine the speeches he had delivered over the previous six years. Impatient with the constant entreaties, he protested that if there were uneasy people, why didn't they "*read* what I have already said?" He repeatedly complained that his views were garbled in the press, and urged that a careful reading of his earlier statements would dispel all their fears and misunderstandings. There was nothing more to be said. To speak out, he wrote, would mean that he had changed his mind, and, he noted, "I am not at liberty to shift my ground."[27]

What Lincoln did not appreciate was that his speeches did not

---

in Lincoln Papers, Library of Congress. Similar appeals were made by Lyman Trumbull, December 14, 1860, and Nathan Sargent, December 12, 1860 (see Lincoln Papers). Even Lyman Trumbull questioned Lincoln's silence and wondered "whether if you have the means of strengthening our friends South, without conceding anything, it might not be proper to do so." Trumbull preferred that Republicans "meet the disunionists and vindicate our position rather than suffer Douglas and northern Democrats to do it." Trumbull to Lincoln, December 14, 1860, in Lincoln Papers.

26. Lincoln to George T. M. Davis, October 27, 1860, Lincoln to Truman Smith, November 10, 1860, Lincoln to George D. Prentice, October 29, 1860, Lincoln to William S. Speer, October 23, 1860, in *Collected Works,* IV, 132–33, 138–39, 134–35, 130; Segal, ed., *Conversations with Lincoln,* 36.

27. Response to Serenade, May 18, 1860, Lincoln to George T. M. Davis, October 27, 1860, Lincoln to Nathaniel P. Paschall, November 16, 1860, in *Collected Works,* IV, 50, 132–33, 139–40. At the same time that he referred people to his speeches, Lincoln in "confidential" correspondence denied that he was pledged to the ultimate extinction of slavery, that he believed the "black man to be the equal of the white,

calm Southern uneasiness; on the contrary, they increased it. In the first place, few of his speeches were readily available to Southern readers. Some campaign biographies included a careful selection but these had little circulation in the South. The publication of the Lincoln-Douglas debates as a Republican campaign document made available some of Lincoln's better-known efforts, but they were designed to destroy Douglas' credibility rather than to address the concerns of the South. And the most famous of Lincoln's utterances during the 1858 campaign, the "House Divided" speech, did nothing to soothe Southern feelings. Some turned to the *Congressional Globe* and Lincoln's speeches in the House of Representatives for enlightenment, but found little there that was relevant to 1860. Lincoln's record, observed one editor, "brief as it is, is to his disadvantage."

In an open letter to Lincoln two weeks after the election, the editor of a St. Louis paper voiced what many were thinking:

> You tell us that you are a conservative man, that your administration would be conducted with reference to the best interests of the whole country— and you cite us to your speeches as enunciating the principles upon which your official course will be based. So say all your friends, Mr. LINCOLN. But we warn you that they will not satisfy fifteen States of the Union now, nor in the future. They ask, and they have a right to ask, new pledges and new guarantees.

Lincoln was not persuaded. "If I go into the Presidency," he told a reporter, "they will find me as I am on record—nothing less, nothing more. My declarations have been made to the world without reservation. They have often been repeated; and now, self-respect demands of me and of the party that has elected me that . . . I should be silent."[28]

When Lincoln stood on his past record, "nothing less, nothing more," he stood also on the one statement with which his name was

---

unqualifiedly," and that he had ever stigmatized Southern whites as immoral and un-Christian. He was clearly drawing some very fine and subtle distinctions. Lincoln to Henry J. Raymond, December 18, 1860, in *Collected Works*, IV, 156.

28. Charleston *Mercury*, May 30, October 30, 1860; Charleston *Courier*, November 10, 1860; Washington *Constitution*, May 26, 19, 1860; Nathaniel P. Paschall to Lincoln, November 18, 1860, in Lincoln Papers, Library of Congress; St. Louis *Daily Missouri Republican*, November 21, 1860, in Dumond, ed., *Southern Editorials on Secession*, 260; Segal, ed., *Conversations with Lincoln*, 43.

most closely linked, and which more than any other utterance classified him as a radical on the slavery question—the "House Divided" speech. Lincoln called it the greatest speech he ever made. Although he conceded that its sentiments could be viewed as an expression of hostility toward the South, he said he never intended to "embitter" Southern feelings. Nevertheless, to Southerners, it seemed to sound the death-knell of their way of life. The keynote was Lincoln's expression of the irrepressible conflict doctrine, four months before Seward popularized the phrase. When coupled with his insistence that slavery violated God's moral law, it sounded dangerously like the "higher law" declarations of the abolitionists. When Lincoln said that the government could not endure permanently half-slave and half-free and that a crisis would soon determine whether the nation would become all slave or all free, Southerners saw only a call for the violent overthrow of slavery. The 1860 election, they feared, was the crisis Lincoln had predicted; with his nomination for the presidency, his warning had become a self-fulfilling prophecy. What Lincoln really meant, declared a Mississippi paper, was that "slavery must be abolished in the slave states, or the government and the Union must be overthrown."

Lincoln's inflexible opposition to the spread of slavery and his conviction that by restricting slavery, the institution would be placed in a condition of ultimate extinction in the Southern states, raised the specter of abolition even more. Lincoln's doctrine, it was said, meant the "total extinction" of the South itself. If Lincoln had been correct in his speeches when he said that slavery was an evil in direct violation of the principles upon which the republic had been founded, then nothing could prevent him from using all his power as president to "eradicate the evil and restore the Government to its 'ancient faith.'" Having invoked "a just God" against slavery, could it be expected that as president he would not exert all the powers of the government "to vindicate what he conceives to be the justice of God?" There was no doubt, wrote J. D. B. De Bow, that once Lincoln was in the White House, he would be "bound by his own arguments and doctrines as the real author of the higher law and irrepressible conflict."[29]

29. Richmond *Enquirer*, May 22, 1860; Segal, ed., *Conversations with Lincoln*, 86; Jackson *Weekly Mississippian*, March 20, 1860, quoted in Reynolds, *Editors Make War*,

With the election returns safely counted and his triumph secure, Lincoln made one indirect concession to those who asked for some new pledge: he wrote a brief paragraph to be inserted in a speech Lyman Trumbull was to deliver at a "Grand Republican Jubilee" in Springfield on November 20. In convoluted prose, reflecting the care with which he chose his words, Lincoln wrote that "all of the States will be left in as complete control of their own affairs respectively, and at as perfect liberty to choose, and employ, their own means of protecting property, and preserving peace and order within their respective limits, as they have ever been under any administration." In other words, Lincoln would not interfere directly with slavery in the states where it existed. The Southern disunionists, he charged, were to blame for having deceived the people into thinking that "their homes, and firesides, and lives" were in danger. He was confident that his statement would end the persistent misrepresentation of the Republican position.

It was only a halfhearted effort, and it did not work. Trumbull spoke Lincoln's words, assured that the Southern mind must now be satisfied. It was not. For one thing, Lincoln's words did not address the heart of the issue that lay between the Republicans and the South, and surely Lincoln knew it. Furthermore, he weakened the effect of his words with his jibe at the disunionists. Finally, Trumbull himself completed the job of undermining Lincoln's effort when he followed with an inflammatory statement of his own. The Constitution, he declared, was not a "slavery-extending instrument"; under Lincoln's leadership the government's policy would favor freedom over slavery, and freedom would be the "law of the territories." Trumbull then denounced secession as terrorism, declared Southern grievances to be "all imaginary," and promised swift and firm action against those who would resist the government. "Woe to the traitors," Trumbull warned, "who are marshaled against it." Hardly words that would soothe Southern feelings.

Trumbull's speech received close attention in the South, for it was assumed he spoke for Lincoln. His language was viewed as tantamount to an "open declaration of war." Lincoln missed the point

---

23; Milledgeville (Ga.) *Federal Union*, December 18, 1860; Washington *Constitution*, July 7, 1860; *De Bow's Review*, XXIX (December, 1860), 798.

entirely, for he could not understand why the South was not happy with his statement. In an "I-told-you-so" fashion, he felt he had made an honest effort to address Southern concerns, but that Southerners had paid no attention to what he said. He believed himself vindicated in his conviction that his strategy of silence had been right, and that nothing he could say would satisfy the South.[30]

Did Lincoln really misunderstand the nature of the crisis that faced the nation following the election? It was inconceivable, even to some of his supporters, that he should be unaware of the seriousness of the danger that threatened the Union, yet he remained persistently silent. Douglas speculated that Lincoln did not yet realize that he was president-elect and "that the shadow he casts is any bigger now than it was last year." Mentally, he was still in Springfield.

Writing from the Illinois capital less than a month before secession became a fact, the young newspaper correspondent Henry Villard felt perplexed at Lincoln's attitude. "Stubborn facts of the most fearful portent," he wrote, were developing at an alarming rate. There was no way that Lincoln could escape them. "He could not possibly shut his eyes to their growing gravity," Villard continued. "He could not block his mind to their serious logic. Every newspaper he opened was filled with clear indications of an impending national catastrophe. Every mail brought him written, and every hour verbal, entreaties to abandon his paralyzed silence, repress untimely feelings of delicacy, and pour the oil of conciliatory conservative assurances upon the turbulent waves of Southern excitement." Yet, as late as mid-February, 1861, after seven slave states had seceded and almost two weeks after the Montgomery convention met to organize the Confederate States of America, Lincoln still insisted that the crisis was "altogether an artificial crisis. . . . Let it alone and it will go down of itself."[31]

30. Passage Written for Lyman Trumbull's Speech at Springfield, Illinois, November 20, 1860, in *Collected Works*, IV, 141–42; Springfield *Illinois State Journal*, November 21, 1860; Washington *Constitution*, November 23, 1860; Lincoln to Henry J. Raymond, November 28, 1860, in *Collected Works*, IV, 145–46.

31. F. Lauriston Bullard, ed., *The Diary of a Public Man, and a Page of Political Correspondence, Stanton to Buchanan* (New Brunswick, N.J., 1946), 55; Henry Villard, *Lincoln on the Eve of '61: A Journalist's Story*, ed. Harold G. Villard and Oswald Garri-

To one Southerner, Lincoln's very silence spoke louder than any words he might utter or any declaration he might make. It was the abolitionist press, he reminded his readers, that was most insistent that Lincoln make no public statements. "Mr. Lincoln has decided the question himself," he concluded, "and he has decided it in accordance with the advice of his Abolition allies." There was no need for Lincoln to declare his policy, for the "party that elected him would not have done so if they thought he would cheat them." On the contrary, if he had declared that his administration would protect the rights of the South "as understood by the Southern people," he would have been treated with "universal contempt" by Republicans.

The charge of partisanship bothered Lincoln, and he took pains to defend himself against it as he traveled to Washington to undertake his presidential duties. "I have not kept silent since the Presidential election from any party wantonness," he told a group in New York City, "or from any indifference to the anxiety that pervades the minds of men about the aspect of the political affairs of the country." Rather, he explained lamely, he had been silent because he thought it proper to be so, and because the "political drama" was changing so rapidly from day to day.

Still, there seems little question that Lincoln's strategy of silence was dictated by strong political and partisan consideration, for he admitted as much on more than one occasion. The "real question" separating the North and South, he suggested, was what he called "Slavery 'propagandism.'" On that question, the Republican party was opposed to the South, and it was there that he also stood. He had been elected by the Republican party, he said, and he intended to sustain that party "in good faith." [32]

That was exactly what the South was afraid of. The Republican party was perceived by Southerners (with considerable justification) as preaching an "unrelenting and bitter hostility to the South." The South was not menaced simply by the fact that Lincoln was elected;

---

son Villard (New York, 1941), 23; Speech at Cleveland, Ohio, February 15, 1861, in *Collected Works*, IV, 215–16.

32. New Orleans *Daily Crescent*, November 28, 1860, in Dumond, ed., *Southern Editorials on Secession*, 272–73; Speech at the Astor House, New York City, February 19, 1861, in *Collected Works*, IV, 230–31; Segal, ed., *Conversations with Lincoln*, 62.

that could have been tolerated if it were nothing more than "a mere slipping in of a candidate of one party" who was running against three rival candidates. But Lincoln's election was no accident. The "significant fact," insisted a Richmond paper, was "that the Northern people, by a sectional vote, have elected a president for the avowed purpose of aggressions on Southern rights." The whole Northern mind, it was said, was "contaminated with abolitionism and hostility to the South." Or, as a New Orleans editor put it, the Republican victory was "incontrovertible proof of a diseased and dangerous public opinion all over the North," a harbinger of "further and more atrocious aggressions" to come.[33]

The 1860 election, Southerners argued, marked a "radical and permanent" change in the attitude of the government toward the South and slavery. Already in the minority, the slave states would lose even more power and influence when the lower house of Congress should be reapportioned according to the 1860 census. Lincoln's election made clear that the South no longer had any "political element at the North" upon which it could "place the slightest reliance," and that the Republicans could win a national election simply by winning the North. What was to prevent them from sweeping the North and electing their president again in 1864? In 1868? In every presidential election afterward? Would Southerners *ever* be able to regain their voice in the government? Even before Lincoln's election, its consequences were apparent. The abolition party, warned *De Bow's Review*, will have "permanent control of one branch of the federal government, and will, . . . within the next four or five years, attain in the other a clear and working majority." At that point, the irrepressible conflict predicted by Lincoln and Seward would reach its crisis, when the "north and south would be arrayed as hostile sections in a contest which could end only by the subjugation of one or the other." Southerners, whether they liked it or not, faced an uneasy set of alternatives, between which they felt they must choose: submit to the superior force of the North, and face the extinction, whether immediate or ultimate, of their institutions; or assume the dignity of independent states.

33. Richmond *Enquirer*, July 18, November 19, 1860; New Orleans *Bee*, December 5, 1860, in Dumond, ed., *Southern Editorials on Secession*, 306.

Under these circumstances, what could Lincoln have possibly said that would have overcome these feelings? The conviction that his election signified a broad, dangerous, and immediate threat to the South was ineradicable and irreversible. "No soothing words, or honeyed promises, from the lips of Mr. LINCOLN himself can up-root this conviction," observed a Georgia editor. It did not matter that Lincoln seemed to place the interests of his party above those of his country, as his opponents claimed. Nor did it matter that he misunderstood the dimensions of the crisis and failed to take its signs seriously, as others have argued. And it certainly did not matter that Lincoln himself, and many of his supporters, believed that a Republican victory would end the slavery agitation once and for all, and that the people would set everything to rights. Lincoln, wrote the Georgian, "rides a wave he cannot control or guide."

Douglas' desperate effort to persuade the South that Lincoln would be powerless for evil, unable to do mischief, restrained at every turn, a man more to be pitied than feared, fell on deaf Southern ears. The momentum of sectional conflict and disunion, to which both the North and the South had contributed, was too strong to check. The point of no return had long since been passed. As if to answer Douglas' appeal to Southerners to calm down and bide their time, a New Orleans paper printed the obituary of the Union: "The soul of the Union is dead, and now let its body be buried." [34]

34. Savannah *Republican*, November 14, 1860, in Dumond, ed., *Southern Editorials on Secession*, 248; Richmond *Enquirer*, July 18, 1860; *De Bow's Review*, XXIX (October, 1860), 534; Florence (Ala.) *Gazette*, November 28, 1860, Augusta *Daily Constitutionalist*, November 16, 1860, New Orleans *Daily Crescent*, December 11, 1860, in Dumond, ed., *Southern Editorials on Secession*, 269, 245, 329.

Index